£14.95

Building
Relationships

Titles in the Group Games Series

Group Games
Building Relationships

THORSTEN BOEHNER

Speechmark

Originally published in German by Don Bosco Verlag, München under the title *Spiele, die Beziehung knüpfen*, © Don Bosco Verlag, München 2000.

Published in 2006 by
Speechmark Publishing Ltd, Telford Road, Bicester, Oxon OX26 4LQ, UK
Telephone +44 (0)1869 244644   Facsimile +44 (0)1869 320040
www.speechmark.net

002-5272/Printed in the United Kingdom/1010

British Library Cataloguing in Publication Data

Boehner, Thorsten
   Building relationships. – (Group Games) (A Speechmark practical activity resource)
   1. Group psychotherapy 2. Recreational therapy.
   3. Interpersonal relations
   I. Title
   616.8'9152

ISBN-10: 0 86388 546 2
ISBN-13: 978 0 86388 546 4

Contents

About the Author

Thorsten Boehner was born in 1967 in Bielefeld. An industrial trader by profession, he has a long-standing interest in amateur dramatics groups and has written a number of children's plays and comedies.

Acknowledgements

I would like to take this opportunity to say a special 'thank you' to my daughters, Stefanie and Miriam. I don't think I would have thought of many of the games in this book without them – and I was able to learn new things and recognise what children need as a result of their play and creative ideas.

I would also like to thank the parents who entrusted their children to me – together, we enjoyed many new experiences.

Thank you to Lilo Seelos, the translator

Note: For the purposes of clarity alone, the group facilitator is referred to as 'she' and the group member is referred to as 'he'.

List of Games

Introduction

For many people the fascination of briefly becoming another person and, from behind that façade, experiencing both familiar and unfamiliar feelings and new situations is a good enough reason to put on a mask and slip into someone else's shoes. Role-play and amateur dramatics do not just represent possibilities for a lively, exciting way of filling leisure time, but also present social and educational opportunities:

◆ Awareness of the self and others is sharpened.
◆ Recognition of one's own limits, as well as a sensitivity to the limitations of others, develops.
◆ Teamwork is practised, as players learn to contribute or to hold back to the appropriate degree.
◆ Flexibility increases as people learn to take risks and explore new experiences in a friendly and safe environment.

Whether this collection of over 140 games is used for working with groups of young people to foster contact with others and develop personal and social skills or with amateur dramatics groups, it offers exciting stimuli. Many of the games are exercises recommended by theatre educationalists and trained actors. When groups meet on a regular basis, exercises that will optimise each session are particularly important. The activities described in this book can be used for regular meetings as well as intensive programmes (seminars, workshops) lasting a number of days.

The games aim to help each individual person to learn their own role, but, more importantly, to get to know themselves and the other group members better. This is particularly important since participating in a group is also about teamwork, and the act of 'working together' is a critical factor. In addition, while using these exercises, every individual group member should begin to recognise and maybe even to push his own limits. The activities also provide themes for the group leader, who often has to deal with questions regarding the organisation of the group: what is the best way to lead a group? What needs to be taken into consideration when beginning to organise a group, working through a programme and then bringing everything to a close at the end? Which support aids are needed? And what else needs to be considered?

GUIDELINES FOR USING THE GAMES

Some of the exercises include a list of suggested *materials*. In addition to these *materials*, chairs may also be required.

The book frequently refers to a *group leader*, who is not only responsible for the group sessions but also takes the lead during most of the exercises.

It is difficult to estimate the most appropriate *group size*, because this tends to vary from exercise to exercise. In general, a group size of ten to a maximum of twenty people has proved practicable. If the groups are too small, exercises may be too short – in order to fill the length of a session, the group leader would then have to offer such a large selection of different exercises that players would frequently be forced to adjust from one activity to the next within too short a space of time. The quality of the activity would then suffer due to the high quantity of different exercises. The disadvantage of groups that are too large is equally obvious – the exercises would simply last too long, exceeding any given time-frame, and leaving little, if any, time for discussion.

To carry out these exercises, *rooms* are required that are big enough for the players to spread out during physical work. In addition, many activities require the players to move around the entire room (eg, 'chase' games), which means that plenty of space is crucial. Good ventilation and the facility to darken the room if necessary (eg, for relaxation exercises) are also important.

During any physical exercises involving partners, try to match the *size and weight of the players*. While bearing this in mind, it is also advantageous to mix and match group members who have not had much contact during the course of previous group activities. In this way, different players can get to know each other better.

One of the most important rules is that there should be no *group pressure* at any time. This is particularly important when players do not think that they can do a particular exercise (eg, because of physical limitations or inhibitions). The limitations of individuals should be accepted by the rest of the group. Equally, if someone opts out of an exercise for whatever reason, this should not lead that person to feel negative about the group, or to feel like an outsider, simply because he is responding to his own feelings and taking them seriously.

The latter part of the book provides a range of different tips and advice for *selecting plays and casting*, as well as suggestions for organising a session or seminar.

For many of the exercises, a subsequent group discussion of feelings and points of view is important. It is inevitable that the performances of individual group members will be discussed during such exchanges. Any comments made should be constructive and objective. This does not mean that no adverse comments can be made. For example, if a player's movements during a mime were too small and the others were therefore unable to guess what he was miming, this could be expressed in the following way: 'Your movements were too unclear. That made it difficult to guess your mime'. Comments such as, 'You should have opted out of this exercise!', or 'You are not suited at all to mime', are, of course, totally unacceptable. Mutual fairness should be the goal at all times. This approach also means that group members whose actions are occasionally criticised, albeit in a constructive manner, should try not to take comments from the rest of the group personally and become angry with the critics, or to perceive themselves as losers.

It is inevitable that certain exercises will take a different course from that originally planned. However, this should not call into question the quality of the exercise or the skills of the players. Group members can consider instead whether an unexpected change may have a positive side from which the group may draw conclusions. For example, if, during paired work, two people realise that they cannot get on (for example, in Game 75, *Blind lead*, p87), this should simply be accepted. It is always possible that things may improve at a later stage.

Finally, it should be remembered that the exercises do not always need to be led by the group leader. Other group members can sometimes lead the sessions. In this way the group leader can be more involved in the activities and others, who would normally just follow instructions, can try the role of the leader for themselves.

The Games

Activities to Facilitate Group Bonding

The first step is always the most difficult, and this is particularly true when working intensively with groups. Just as with sports, a good start helps to achieve the best result. This chapter aims to make the beginning of group sessions much easier, especially for newly formed groups. Using the following games, group members can gradually become closer to and more familiar with each other.

1) Greetings with a stone

All of the group members sit together in a circle. As soon as the group leader has said a few words to welcome the group, she passes a stone (ideally about the size of a fist) around the circle. The key rule is that only the person holding the stone is allowed to speak: interruptions by other group members are forbidden. The person holding the stone should tell the others something about himself. In this way, invite everyone to voice their expectations and talk about how they feel when approaching the new group. Everybody else should listen to the stone holder. This strengthens attention and mutual respect.

Materials: fist-sized stone

2   Greetings in a circle

All the players sit in a circle and an empty chair is placed in the middle. Individual players take it in turn to sit on the chair and talk about their expectations with regard to the forthcoming group session. When they have finished they return to their original place. The person to their left has the next turn.

Some people may feel uncomfortable sitting in the middle and being the focus of attention. If in doubt, Game 1, *Greetings with a stone*, is a good alternative.

(3) Greetings from the centre

The group stands in a circle. One player at a time steps into the middle and wishes the rest of the group 'good morning' or 'good evening', depending on the time of day. Everybody does so in their own individual way: loudly, quietly, in a good or bad mood, in a tired or lively way. Players can also choose their own greeting, perhaps saying, 'Well, hello everybody', 'Nice to see you all', and so on. Once an individual has given their greeting, they take up their original place within the circle. Then the whole group steps forward into the centre together and repeats the greeting, using the same words and, if possible, the same tone of voice and intonation.

4 Ball-name game

Group members who do not know each other very well often find that one of their biggest problems is remembering everybody's name. This can be helped by an activity which should immediately follow the initial greetings. The players stand in a circle. The group leader has a ball which she throws to another player while saying her own name. The other player catches the ball and then calls out their own first name while throwing the ball to someone else. That person calls out their name and throws the ball to a fourth person, and so on. The pace should increase as the game goes on.

Game variation

A variation of the game is for the person throwing the ball to call out the name of the person they are throwing the ball to.

Materials: ball – anything from a tennis ball to a football is suitable

(5) What does my name mean?

Use a book of names to find out more about the original meaning of people's forenames. Some people may already know that 'Tariq' means 'night visitor', 'Sylvia' means 'person of the forest' and 'Catherine' means 'pure'. Many players will make surprising discoveries, because the majority of people only know the meaning of their own name, if that.

Materials: book of names, obtainable in any library

6 Name – description – movement

The group stands in a circle. The group leader steps into the middle and calls out her name, preceded by an adjective (for example, 'Jolly Jan'), which need not necessarily correspond to her character or current mood. She accompanies this with any sort of body movement, for example, waving a hand, and then returns to her place in the circle. The whole group then steps into the middle and repeats what the group leader has just said ('Jolly Jan'), while also copying the body movement shown by the group leader. Then the circle reforms and the player on the left of the group leader has the next turn. He steps into the middle and says his name, preceded by an adjective (for example, 'Miserable Marcus'), and makes a body movement, such as a knee-bend. Once he has returned to his place in the circle, all of the players once again step into the middle and repeat what they have heard and seen. The game continues until everybody has had a turn.

7 My name does the rounds

The group stands in a circle. The first player turns to his neighbour on the right, and introduces himself, saying, for example, 'My name is John!' (but using his own name), and shaking his neighbour's hand. The person who is being greeted responds by saying loudly and clearly, 'Hello, John!' 'John' then moves around the circle, introducing himself to each person in turn. Once 'John' has introduced himself to everybody in the circle he returns to his original place and the person to his right then introduces himself in the same way to all the other players. During this activity it is important that the players greeting each other maintain eye contact.

(8) Name signs

This is a good variation for recently formed groups whose members are not yet familiar with each other. Prior to the next meeting, each player makes a sign with their own name on it. On the sign the players should write not just their names, but also a symbol or object that is in some way linked to them as a person. A sports enthusiast could draw a football on his name sign, another person might paste a small picture of his personal hero onto his, the next person might draw his favourite food, and so on. At the time of the next meeting, everybody attaches their name sign to their chest, and the group sits together. One at a time, players explain why they have chosen a particular symbol or picture.

Materials: paper, colouring pens, small strips of double-sided sticky tape for attaching the name signs

9) I say your name

Group members get together in pairs, with the partners facing each other. Player A repeats the name of player B several times, while continuously changing his facial expression and intonation. B watches A carefully, so he can comment on A's performance afterwards. Then B says A's name in different variations. The partners should swap roles several times during this game.

10 Group puzzle

Take a group photograph when a new group forms. Prior to a meeting, the group leader has the photo enlarged to a size which will suit this activity. She cuts up the enlarged photo into as many pieces as there are group members. Each photo piece is placed inside an envelope and at the beginning of the meeting each player is handed an envelope. The players then open their envelopes and take out the photo piece. The individual pieces are placed on the floor and have to be put together to recreate the original photo. Apart from the enjoyment derived from the game, something that is true for each group will become clear: a recognisable result can only be achieved if everybody contributes their 'bit'.

Materials: enlarged group photo, scissors, envelopes

(11) Sharing secrets

The players get together in pairs. They then confide to each other a personal detail that is not generally known to the rest of the group or to many other people. With a group that has not met before this could be about jobs, hobbies, favourite foods, or favourite artist, actor, singer, and so on. Afterwards the group gets together in a circle and has to guess the information about individual group members.

For example, in a group that has not met before, Julia and Max get together. The group leader has requested that group members talk about their hobbies. Julia tells Max that she likes to play tennis. Max reveals to Julia that he loves cooking.

When all the player pairs have consulted one another, and Julia and Max's turn comes round, Julia tells the group, 'The person sitting next to me is Max. I wonder what his hobby is? Is it a) sailing, b) cooking, or c) bowling?' The other group members now have to guess the answer. Once the group has agreed on one of the three possibilities, Max tells them his real hobby. Then he introduces Julia and names three potential hobbies for her – again the group has to guess the real one.

Game variation

People who already know each other could guess mischief they caused as children, such as scribbling on walls or letting the air out of a car tyre. Remind the group members not to reveal intimate secrets that have no place in such a group.

(12) Interview

This game is another way in which group members can get to know each other better. The group divides into pairs. Each partner then tells the other something about himself – his job, his hobby, little quirks, and so on. Afterwards the group forms a circle and two chairs are placed side by side in the middle. In turn, the individual interview pairs sit in the chairs and introduce one another. Player A introduces player B to the other people in the circle, and briefly describes what he has just learned about B. After that it is B's turn to talk about A.

Game variation

As a variation, everybody could try to role-play their interview partner, talking in the first person about the things they have found out. The round has finished when every interview pair has introduced each other.

(13) Raffle

Prior to the session it is agreed that everybody brings in a small object which may look insignificant to the others, but which, for whatever reason, has some sort of special meaning for the person concerned. A big fabric bag is put in the meeting room, into which everybody places their object, ideally in a way that prevents the others from seeing what the object is. After that, the group leader walks around the room with the bag, and everybody takes out an object without looking. If anybody chooses their own object, they put it back and try again. The group then gets together and each person talks about what the object in their hands makes them think of – perhaps saying what impression the object makes on them and what they imagine the owner of the object to be like. After every player has made a comment, everybody reclaims their own object and, during a new round, the true owners relate something about the meaning of their particular objects.

Game variation

In a variation on this game, only half of the group places its objects into the bag and each member of the second half takes one out. Afterwards each member of the second group pairs up with the owner of the object he has pulled out of the bag.

Materials: a fabric bag, one small object per player

---

14 Childhood photos

This game can be played by groups whose members already know one another, as well as by groups who are not yet familiar with each other. Each player agrees to bring in a photograph that shows him as a child. Childhood photographs depicting the players between the ages of five and ten are most suitable. The group leader collects all of the photographs and puts each one into an identical envelope. The envelopes are shuffled, and each player picks one. If anybody ends up with their own photograph, he has to draw again. Then each player tries to find the person whose photograph they are holding. Afterwards, comparisons can be made: who has changed a great deal, and who still has some of their childhood characteristics?

Game variation

As in Game 13, *Raffle*, this game can also be used to make up pairs. One half of the group gives its photographs to the group leader, who puts them into envelopes. Each person from the other half of the group picks an envelope, then pairs up with the person shown on the photo.

Materials: one childhood photograph and envelope per player

15 Key experience

If groups have been working together for a long time there is a danger that the same group members will associate with each other during and after group activities. This might begin with the seating order. If the group forms a circle – even just for a greeting round – it is very likely that the same people will end up sitting next to each other every time. Right from the start this makes it harder to get to know other group members better. This game helps alleviate the problem. Initially, the players choose their own positions in a circle of chairs, but the group leader stands in the centre. She approaches a player, reaches out her hand and says, 'Good evening …', followed by the name of that player. The person addressed gets up and, together with the group leader, approaches a third person, who is greeted by both in the same way and also gets up. The game continues until all of the players are on their feet. Then the group leader noisily drops a bunch of keys on the floor. This is the sign for everybody to sit down – however, because the group leader also wants to sit down, there will be one chair too few. The person who is left without a chair picks up the bunch of keys and starts a new greetings round, following the same process as before. Whatever else happens, the previous seating order will be completely changed.

Materials: bunch of keys

16 Travel bug

As in Game 15, *Key experience*, Games 16, 17 and 18 are all about breaking habits and reshaping the group. Again, everybody sits on a chair in a circle and the group leader stands in the centre. Then each player is named for a town or city (eg, London, Birmingham, Liverpool, Cambridge, Oxford, Watford, etc). The group leader calls out a travel route – for example, 'I am driving from Birmingham to Oxford, and I am going now!' On this, the two players concerned have to swap seats – but they have to watch out, because the group leader is after one of their seats. If the leader manages to get a seat, the player left without one becomes the new route organiser. Otherwise the group leader has to try her luck again. The whole game can become even more active if the player in the middle incorporates several towns into the route – for example, 'I am driving from Canterbury to Liverpool, via London, Watford and Birmingham, and I am going now!' Now all of the players whose towns have been named have to try to swap seats. Once again, only a very few players will still be sitting in their original places at the end. In this way, the players are encouraged to swap and make contact with other players and, in the process, they develop their concentration.

17 Swapping on cue

This is a third seat-swapping game. The group members are sitting on chairs in a circle, with the group leader standing in the centre. A cue word is agreed (eg, summer), which, during the course of the game, will give the signal for change. The group leader then starts to tell a story into which, at some point, she will incorporate the word 'summer'. On hearing the cue, all of the players have to swap seats and the group leader also has to try to sit down. The person who is left without a chair now has to choose a new cue and tell a new story, until another change of seats is triggered.

18 Port and starboard

The group sits on chairs pushed close together to form a circle, with one chair left empty. In the middle there is a volunteer – the 'captain'. The captain now directs the players by commanding them to move one position to the right or left. When the captain calls out 'starboard', the player who has an empty chair to their right has to quickly move on to that chair and the players on his left follow suit. Equally, when the captain calls out 'port', the players have to move to the left in the same way. Moving from chair to chair has to happen quickly, because the captain will also try to sit down on an empty chair. If the captain manages to sit down, the person who is left without a chair has to go into the centre and play the role of captain.

Before starting the game, give the players a few minutes to practise discriminating between starboard (right) and port (left).

Warm-up Activities

This section contains exercises predominantly designed for warming up the body. Players who are mentally tense and feel inhibited in making contact with others or in coming out of their shells are often also physically tense. Therefore this chapter focuses specifically on warming up different body parts, from head to toe. At the same time these exercises also contribute to developing concentration.

19 Head-to-toe warm-up

Everyone starts this exercise by using their hands to stroke their faces firmly, from the centre outwards. The 'wiped-off' tiredness is then thrown to the floor with a decisive hand movement. Then everybody makes exaggerated facial expressions: raising the eyebrows; opening the eyes and mouth as wide as possible; and spreading the nostrils. After a few seconds, the facial muscles are tensed: the eyes are squeezed closed tightly, the forehead is wrinkled; the lips are pressed together; and then, a few seconds later, the facial muscles are released once more. Then the group pats their shoulders, upper and lower arms and stomach. While doing this, they should take as much time as they need, until they feel that their body is indeed 'patted awake'. Then the arms are stretched forward: the fingers are spread out as much as possible and then screwed up into a fist, before they are spread out again once more. Since it is difficult to pat one's own back 'awake', get everyone to stand in a circle, one behind the other, and thoroughly, but gently, pat the back of their neighbour, taking care around the area of the spine. Then each individual can pat their own upper and lower thighs. In order to 'wake up' the feet, everybody sits down on the floor and begins to thoroughly knead first their left and then their right foot with their hands. Attention should be paid to all parts of the foot: the toes, soles, uppers and sides, and the heel. At the end, everybody should 'listen' to their own bodies and treat again any parts of the body that, in their opinion, are not warm enough yet.

20 Warming up to music

The players walk through the room to the beat of fast music. The walk should be varied: forwards, backwards, on tiptoe, on the heels, on the outside and inside of the feet, with small or big steps, jumping, and so on. During this, the remaining body parts should not be forgotten: the head, shoulders and arms should be shaken occasionally to release tension.

Materials: CD player or tape recorder and fast piece of music

21) Warming up with music and dance

The group stands in a circle and starts to dance to the music. One after the other, the players move into the middle of the circle and dance in their own individual way; if necessary, another player can be invited to dance with them. The others copy the dance modelled by the person in the middle without making fun of it – every individual style of dancing should be accepted. Then the first person leaves the middle of the circle, and the next dancer moves into the centre to model their dance. The game continues until everybody has had a turn.

Materials: CD player or tape recorder and fast piece of music

22 Kicking balloons

Each player ties an inflated balloon to his ankle using string. Once the group leader gives the signal to begin, everybody tries to burst each other's balloons by stamping on them. Obviously the group members have to keep an eye on their own balloon at the same time, to try to prevent it from being burst. The winner is the last person still to have an inflated balloon left on their ankle.

Game variation
To vary the game, give the players two balloons, one for each foot.

Materials: lots of balloons and string

(23) Chair relay

The players form two teams, and the leader of each sits on one of two chairs that have been placed next to each other. The other players sit on chairs placed in a long row behind their own team leader, leaving an alley between the two rows of chairs wide enough for one person to walk down. At the signal to begin, both leaders jump up and run along their team's row to the last player in the line, giving this person a light pat on the back. This player now has to get up, while the leader sits down on his empty chair. The player who was previously last in the row now gives the person in front of him (ie, the last-but-one player) the command to get up and make room by patting him on the back. The last-but-one player gets up and pats the back of the person in front of him. The whole process continues until the second player in the row of chairs sits at the front of the line. Then he gets up, runs back to the person who used to be the leader (who now sits right at the back of the row), pats him on the back, and the moving-up process continues until the original leader is once again sitting on the first chair in the row, just as at the beginning of the game.

The catcher chases the pack

One person is chosen to be the catcher. The catcher now has to try to catch another person in the group, but this is made more difficult by the rule that he is not allowed to catch the others if they have teamed up with someone else by holding hands. The catcher has to leave these pairs alone and turn his attention to the players who are still running around individually. Partnerships have to dissolve as soon as the catcher is out of reach. If the catcher is successful, the person who has been caught becomes the new catcher.

Game variation
The game can be made more difficult for the people being chased by ruling that in order to be safe from the catcher they have to get together in groups of three, or even four, rather than just in twos.

(25) Snake hunt

All of the players stand in a row one behind the other, and put their hands on the waist of the person in front of them. Standing like this they form a snake, with the first player representing the head of the snake, and the last player its tail. At a signal the group runs forward, with the 'head' determining the direction, and has to try to catch the 'tail'. The players are not allowed to let go of each other while doing this.

Game variation

To vary the game, two snakes are formed. The head of one snake has to try to catch the tail of the other snake and vice versa without letting their own tail being caught.

26 Throwing a ball and counting

Any lightweight ball, such as a tennis ball or a larger plastic ball, can be used for this game. The players stand in a circle and throw the ball to each other. The group leader counts the throws. If the players get up to 50 without dropping the ball on the floor, this means that they have concentrated well.

This exercise sounds a lot easier than it is. During the first attempts, the ball is likely to be dropped before reaching 10 throws. But do not give up – it gets easier!

Game variation

Well-practised groups can try this experiment with two or even three balls. However, they should leave out the counting – the aim is merely that the balls do not touch the floor.

Materials: tennis ball or another lightweight ball

27 Goal wall

The group divides into two teams that sit facing each other alongside opposite walls of the room. Group A is given a tennis ball. One player in Group A now has to try to roll the ball between the players in Group B, so that it hits the wall behind them. If a player in Group B catches the ball before it hits the wall, it is that player's turn. He now has to try to hit the wall opposite his team by aiming the ball through a gap in Group A. One point is given every time a player is successful. It is important to emphasise that the players are only allowed to roll the ball, not to throw it. In addition, all of the players have to remain seated, never getting up or moving away from their places to catch a ball. They are only allowed to stretch out their arms and legs to stop it. The game is over when one group scores a previously agreed number of points. This exercise aims to train the ability to defend one's own area.

Materials: tennis ball

28 Chair football

Chair football is another good game for practising defending one's own area (see also Game 27, *Goal wall*). The group forms two teams. The players of each team sit on a row of chairs, with the two rows facing each other at a distance of about 3m apart. The group leader rolls a ball along the corridor between the two rows. Each player has to try to score a goal, using only their feet. The goals are the spaces between the chair legs of the opposite team, as well as the gaps between their chairs. The gaps should be of a size that allows the players sitting next to each other to just touch the tips of their toes when they stretch their legs out to the side. As soon as a goal has been scored, the leader takes the ball back and then rolls it again along the corridor. The team who first scores a previously agreed number of goals is the winner.

Materials: football

29) The treasure in the chalk circle

Using chalk, the leader draws a circle, approximately 6m in diameter, on the floor. Inside that circle she draws another circle, approximately 3m in diameter. The small circle represents the castle inside which a 'treasure' is placed, in the form of a pyramid made from cans. Four people (the 'guardians') are positioned around the small circle to guard the treasure, but they are not allowed to cross into its centre. The rest of the players (the 'attackers') are standing around the edge of the big circle. They now have to try to hit the treasure by throwing small balls. The guardians must try to prevent this, fending off any of the balls thrown by the attackers. The attacker with the most hits wins the game. Afterwards, some of the attackers can swap roles with the guardians.

Materials: chalk, cans, small balls

30 Group formation with music

This exercise can be used to monitor and improve reactions. Players pair up and walk through the room, accompanied by music. The leader stops the music at any point and calls out a number, for example, 'Five!' The pairs now have to get together in groups of five as quickly as possible. As five is an odd number, obviously some of the pairs will be forced to split up. It is interesting to observe which pairs split up immediately and which pairs stay together waiting for others to take the initiative to join them. Those people who do not manage to form a group of five are out. The remaining players form pairs again and walk through the room to music, until the leader calls out a new number.

Materials: CD player or tape recorder and fast piece of music

31) Back and forth

One person goes into the middle, while the others make a circle of chairs around him. The player in the middle now approaches any one person in the surrounding circle, pointing to his mouth and saying, for example, 'This is my stomach!' Then he counts aloud from one to ten. The player who has been addressed now quickly has to give the appropriate reverse response, in this case by pointing to his own stomach and stating, 'This is my mouth!' If he is unable to do this by the time his opponent has counted to ten, the player in the centre is allowed to sit down. The loser has to go into the centre himself and try to get a chair again.

In order to win back his chair, the player can increase the level of difficulty by turning to one of the players in the circle, pointing to his left eye, and claiming, 'This is my right foot!' Logically, the person addressed now has to point to their left foot and say, 'This is my right eye!' – but again, this has to happen before the player in the middle has counted to ten.

32 Yes-no game

The players form a circle. The group leader turns to her neighbour on the left and calls out to him, loudly and clearly, 'Yes'. She supports this 'yes' with a hand gesture, namely, holding out her hands, flat and open, towards her neighbour. The neighbour addressed now has two choices: he can accept the 'yes' and pass it on to the neighbour on his own left, with a loud 'yes', accompanied by the same hand gesture, or he can reject the 'yes' by crossing his arms in front of his chest and responding to the leader with a loud 'no'. If he chooses 'no', the leader still has to try to get rid of her 'yes' in the same way, approaching the neighbour on her *right* this time. That person can then either pass it on to the neighbour on their own right, or also reject it. If her 'yes' is rejected for a second time, the leader has to try her luck again with the person on her *left*.

This game works best if, for the first two rounds, everybody accepts the 'yes' played to them by their neighbour and passes it on. Then the 'no' can be introduced into the game, so that the game changes direction. Anybody hesitating for too long over whether to accept or reject the 'yes' is out. Equally, anybody who accompanies his 'yes' or 'no' with either the wrong hand gesture or none at all is also out. The aim of this game is simply for players to learn to follow their first impulse. So if that impulse is 'yes', then this should be shown clearly. The same goes for 'no'.

33) Forming and clapping sentences

This game is great for assessing and developing the level of concentration within the group.

The players sit or stand in a circle. Each player is allocated particular letters, which he has to remember. X and Z have been excluded from this simplified example for four players.

Player 1 is given	A, E, I, M, Q, U
Player 2 is given	B, F, J, N, R, V
Player 3 is given	C, G, K, O, S, W
Player 4 is given	D, H, L, P, T, Y

The players now have to clap a given word, each clapping only the letters that have been allocated to them. For example, the group leader might give the word 'circle', and the players then have to clap in the following sequence:

Player 3	C
Player 1	I
Player 2	R
Player 3	C
Player 4	L
Player 1	E

Game variation

Not that difficult? Try moving on to the next round, in which the players have to clap whole sentences, such as, 'This morning it was raining in London'. When clapping sentences the players also need to agree who is going to clap the 'space' between the end of one word and the beginning of the next.

34 Group counting

The players spread out anywhere in the room – they do not even have to be immediately visible to each other. Then everyone tries to count from one to twenty, with the group leader starting the game by saying 'one', and waiting. After a brief pause, any other player may call out 'two'. Then another player calls out 'three', and so on, until the number 20 is reached. It will be obvious that several players at a time may have the urge to call out the next number, which is the point of this game. Individual group members have to be very sensitive to the rest of the group to ensure they only call out the correct number when they are certain that no other group member is about to do the same. If two or more players call out a number at the same time the game must start again, with the group leader once again beginning at 'one'.

It is important not to rush this exercise, as experience has shown that the game requires several attempts to flow successfully.

35   Never say 'yes' or 'no'

Each player is given five playing cards, or similar objects which could be swapped. Everybody now finds a partner at random, and these pairs engage in conversation. During this, each player tries to get the other player to say the words 'yes' or 'no', for example, by asking trick questions, such as, 'Can I have your card?', or 'Shall we stop now?' If a player says 'yes' or 'no' by mistake, he has to hand over a card to his partner. Both then have to find another partner. In this way, new partnerships are created continuously. The winner is the person who, when the game ends, has the most cards.

Materials: a large number of playing cards, or similar objects such as counters or buttons

(36) Nouns in rhythm

Everybody stands in a circle and the group leader models a three-part movement: she could, for example, stamp her foot, slap her hand on her thigh and then click her fingers. To start with, everybody simply copies this sequence in rhythm.

Then a new round starts. As before, everybody stamps their feet and slaps their hands on their thighs, but during the clicking the leader says a certain letter, such as 'R'. At the next click, her neighbour on the left has to give a noun that begins with that letter (such as 'raisin') and then say a new letter at the next click – perhaps 'G'. At the next click, the neighbour to his left has to call out a suitable noun, such as 'garden'. The game continues around the circle in the same way. Anybody who cannot decide on a new letter or a suitable noun while keeping the rhythm has to leave the circle.

(37) What is that?

All of the players sit in a circle of chairs. The group leader gives a playing card to each of her neighbours on the left and right. While doing this, she says to the neighbour on her right, 'This is a car!', and to the neighbour on her left, 'This is a banana!' Both neighbours now ask the leader, 'What is that?' The leader answers, 'A car', to the person on her right and, 'A banana', to the person on her left. Both neighbours then pass on the cards to their own neighbours, with the words, 'This is a car!' and 'This is a banana!' The recipients of the cards ask in return 'What is that?' However, from now on, the answer must not be given immediately – instead the question has to be relayed by each of the previous players in turn back to the leader. The leader's answers to the right (a car) and to the left (a banana) also have to travel back around the circle, until they get to the person who last asked the question, 'What is that?' The cards continue to be passed around the circle and will obviously cross over at some stage. This point in the game demands particular concentration. At the end, the group leader should be holding both cards in her hands again.

Materials: two different playing cards

(38) Contact game

This exercise subdivides into three stages. During the first phase, all of the players walk around the room and, at intervals of a few seconds, they jump up into the air near a wall, clap one hand against the wall and call out, 'Ha!' Once they have done this a few times, the second phase begins. During this phase, the players briefly make physical contact with another person in the room (for example, by tapping another person's shoulder with their index finger), while also calling out, 'Ha!', as if they are trying to frighten their fellow player. After a few minutes, the third phase begins. In this, every player must address another player crossing his path as he walks around the room. He should engage the other player in a short conversation by saying, 'Hi, how are you?', 'Nice day today!', and so on – but he must move on after a maximum of three sentences, while saying, 'I'm sorry, I've got to go!', and continuing to walk around the room.

Exercises for Building Trust & Awareness

These exercises help to develop the individual's awareness of himself and his physical environment as well as, perhaps most importantly, his sensitivity to his fellow players. They are intended to make the difficult 'getting-to-know-you' process easier. Many of the exercises are best carried out in twos and, as mentioned in the introduction, it is advantageous if those who previously have not had much to do with each other are teamed up. In any case, the aim is to tune in to each other through joint play, even if this attunement only lasts for a session, a set of rehearsals or a seminar.

(39) Sorting by category

Four or five chairs are placed next to each other. One person stands on each chair. Then the group leader asks the players to categorise themselves, for example, by shoe size. The person with the biggest shoe size could stand to the far left and the person with the smallest shoe size could stand to the far right. The players now have to change their chairs so that in the end they are all standing on the chairs in order of shoe size. The special challenge of this game is that they have to do this without saying a word.

Game variations

There are lots of potential variations on this game: try sorting by lightest or darkest eye or hair colour, or height, and so on.

40 Filling the room

At the beginning of the game, the group leader declares the whole of the floor to be a large disc. In order for this imaginary disc not to tip in any particular direction the players must distribute themselves across it, to keep it in balance.

The players spread out, walking all around the room. While doing this they have to make sure that there are no large, unused spaces. This means that as soon as a player notices that there is a sizeable area without other players, he moves into that space. From there he looks out for the next free place in the room and then goes there. Because all of the players will be trying to do this at the same time, there will always be gaps to be filled.

41 Chair – hat – cellphone

The group sits on chairs in a circle with the group leader. To start the game, the leader puts her left hand on her head. This signals that she is wearing a hat. Then she holds her closed right hand to her ear, to indicate that she is using a cellphone. The group leader is now sitting, 'wearing a hat' and 'using a cellphone'. Now it is the group's task to portray the opposite of the group leader's actions. This means that, in the example given, all of the other group members have to stand, with their arms hanging down by their sides, indicating that they are not wearing hats and not using a phone. From then on the group leader can test the group's speed of reaction as much as she likes, for example, by standing up while taking her hand off her head. As soon as the leader makes a move the others have to do the opposite, in this case sit down and put their left hands on their heads. Then the group leader sits back down again, puts her left hand on her head once more and takes away her right hand from her ear. This should trigger the rest of the group to stand up, take their left hands off their head ('removing hats') and put their closed right hands to their ears ('using cellphones'). The game can be continued for as long as you like. The group leader can alter one, two or three things each time she moves.

42 Rock – scissors – paper

Many people will remember this childhood game. The symbols for rock, scissors, and paper are simply represented by making different shapes with the hand: a fist represents a rock; the index and middle fingers spread out represent scissors; and a flat hand represents paper. In contrast to the usual way of playing the game, this version is not about competing against each other, but about finding a common symbol for the whole group to use.

To start with, everyone spreads out randomly around the room. Then they all make fists and punch their hands into the air three times. While doing this, they shout out, 'One, two three!'. On 'three', everybody has to shape their hand into one of the three symbols. It is unlikely that everybody will decide on the same symbol to start with, but they can glance briefly around the room to establish which symbol is favoured by the majority. Then the players make fists, punch the air, call out 'One, two, three!', and form one of the three symbols again. What does the second result look like? Is there a trend towards a particular symbol among the group?

When the players are very perceptive, it sometimes takes only three or four attempts before everyone decides on the same symbol. It is important that no one speaks during the game. The agreement on a common symbol has to take place without words.

43 Cockerel – lion – frog

The group leader asks all of the group members to portray one of the following animals: a cockerel, a lion, or a frog. Then the group leader counts to three, and everyone spontaneously changes into their chosen animal. Some flutter around the room like disturbed cockerels, others parade about with their chests sticking out like lions, and the frogs hop around and get in everyone's way. While they are miming, everyone should observe each other's role-play. As soon as the group leader shouts 'stop', everybody freezes. After a little while, a new round is started and everyone again chooses to portray one of the three animals. This time, as in Game 42, the group has to agree silently on just one animal for everyone to imitate, so that, as soon as possible, the whole group is walking around the room all pretending to be cockerels, lions or frogs.

44 Transformation scene

Two teams are formed and stand in lines, two metres apart, so that each player has an opposite number. In the space of one minute, each person has to memorise as much as possible about the appearance of the player opposite. At the group leader's command, all of the players turn round and stand back-to-back with their opposite number for approximately two minutes. During this time, each person has to change three things about their appearance. Items such as glasses, hats, watches, rings, and so on can be exchanged between players on the same team. After two minutes, everyone turns round again. Now they have to detect what has changed about the person opposite. The players take it in turns to itemise the changes they have noticed in their opposite numbers.

45 Thimble

The group leader explains to everybody present that they have to find a thimble hidden somewhere in the room. All of the players start looking while, unnoticed by the group, the leader sticks a thimble on her finger. Any member of the group who notices the thimble must not tell anyone else, but simply sit down quietly on a chair. The game ends only when all of the players have spotted the thimble and are sitting on chairs.

Materials: thimble

46 Walking in time

All of the players walk around the room. As time goes by, all players aim to walk in time with each other and to maintain this for several minutes.

47 Feeling blindly

Members of the group spread out across the room and close their eyes. The group leader plays some music while the players walk around the room with their hands outstretched. When one hand meets another, a hearty handshake follows, and then the walk continues. When the group leader stops the music, everybody stays with the partner whose hand they are in the process of shaking. Players who do not have a partner when the music stops quickly reach for one. Then the partners feel each other's faces. They should be trying not only to guess each other's identity, but also thoroughly explore the face of the other person and thus to discover things they may not have noticed before. After a while, at a signal from the group leader, everyone opens their eyes again and studies their partner properly.

Materials: tape recorder/CD player and music

(48) Big knot

The group stands in a circle and holds hands. The group leader plays some music. While the music is playing, the group starts moving. Still holding hands to make a chain, people climb over each other or crawl through each other's legs and, this way, form a human 'knot'. When the leader thinks the knot is big enough, she stops the music. Everybody stays still for a moment; then the players try to 'undo' the knot without talking to each other.

(49) Back-to-back

Two players of approximately equal size and weight sit back-to-back on the floor, bend their legs and link arms at the elbow. Now they have to try to get up at the same time without talking to each other. They are successful when both, still hooked up at the elbow, are standing upright. This exercise can also be carried out with more people – perhaps groups of four or eight – whereupon it becomes proportionally more difficult. It is a particularly satisfying feeling for everyone if, towards the end of a seminar or a rehearsal, they all manage to stand up as a group. If they do succeed in doing this, it is evidence that the group has really tuned in to each other during the time they have spent together.

Describing objects

The group leader spreads out a selection of random objects, ideally small enough to hold in the hand, and various players select an object. Then the first player goes into the middle of the room and begins to describe his chosen object, in as much detail as possible, to the other players. He could listen to the object to see whether he can discover a noise coming from it, or he could smell it and feel it with his fingers before describing to the group what the object feels like. It is very important for everyone to be objective in their description. For example, if the object is an old spectacle case, the player could say, 'It feels worn', or 'It smells of leather', and so on. Subjective or emotional comments such as, 'It looks really ugly', are not allowed.

Materials: random selection of small objects

51) I see and I hear

The group gets into pairs to stroll around the room. As they do so, player A in each pair describes for player B what he perceives around him. This could involve auditory signals (noises from outside, voices inside the room), as well as visual perceptions (objects and people in the room). In contrast to Game 50, *Describing objects*, player A is allowed to make subjective comments about the environment (eg, 'The room is too full', 'It is too loud in here'). He could also draw comparisons such as, 'The green carpet reminds me of a summer meadow'. B listens carefully and quietly. After five minutes, the partners swap roles and it is B's turn to talk, while both partners continue to walk around the room.

52 The persuasion game

Two people at a time stand opposite each other, at least five metres apart. One player in the pair now tries to convince his partner to come over to him. To do this, he is only allowed to use the word 'come'. Players can try saying this in all sorts of ways: demanding, hesitating, pleading, and so on. Player B, however, is only allowed to move towards player A if he really has been convinced to move – that is, when he really feels that player A genuinely wants him to walk over to him. How close B chooses to come – a few steps, or directly up to A – is totally B's decision. A has only achieved his aim when B is standing right in front of him.

53) Give me that!

Players get together in pairs. Player A in each pair tries using all sorts of ways to talk B into giving him one of his possessions, such as his watch, necklace, left shoe, glasses or an object that B picked up at the beginning of the game. Player A can try all sorts of tactics to get the object: demanding it; asking for it in a restrained way; a gentle or friendly request; flying off the handle; pleading; begging; asking for it angrily, and so on. When A finally gets the feeling that B cannot be convinced to hand over the desired item, the roles are swapped. The roles must also be swapped if B is talked into handing over the requested item. Afterwards, the players reflect on the point at which a player gave up, or the other player gave in.

Materials: random selection of objects

(54) Take that!

This exercise represents the exact opposite of Game 53, *Give me that!* Again, pairs are formed, but this time player A tries to persuade his partner, B to accept a particular object. This could be a piece of jewellery belonging to A, or an item of clothing (hat, shoe, scarf). When A thinks that B cannot be convinced to accept the item in question, the roles are swapped. The same applies if B gives in and accepts A's item. Afterwards, the players reflect on the point at which a player gave up, or the other player gave in.

Materials: random selection of objects

55 This is an apple

The players organise themselves into pairs. Player A in each pair takes any object that can be found in the room (eg, a pen). He then tries to talk player B into believing that this is a totally different object to the one that he can actually see. For example, player A might point to a pen while looking straight into B's eyes and saying, in an insistent manner, 'This is an apple!' B now tries to retreat from A. Player A's task is to stay with his partner and continue to try to 'sell' him the pen as an apple. After a previously agreed period of time the two players swap roles. Afterwards, both can give their impressions. Did anyone get to the point where they were going to let their partner sell them the real object as something else?

Materials: random selection of objects

56 Letting energy flow

The players sit in a circle on the floor and hold hands with their respective neighbours. The group leader's aim is to let energy flow through the group. She begins by imagining that a stream of energy is going through her own body. This energy starts in her right hand and flows up the arm, through the right shoulder, the head and into the left shoulder. Then the energy goes down her left arm into the left hand. Once it has arrived there, the group leader signals this by gently squeezing the hand of the neighbour on her left. This neighbour then lets the energy flow through his own body in the same manner, passing it on to the neighbour on his left with a gentle hand squeeze.

It is important that not a word is spoken during this exercise. In addition, everybody should close their eyes, so they can concentrate even better on the arrival of the energy, the way it is flowing through their bodies, and passing it on carefully to the next person.

Game variation

If the group is already familiar with this exercise, individual players could sometimes reverse the flow of energy once it has run through their bodies. They could decide not to pass it on to the neighbour on their left, instead letting it flow through their own bodies once more before returning it to the neighbour on their right, from whom they originally received it.

57 Letting tunes flow

The group sits together in a circle, with the players closing their eyes and holding each other's hands. Then the group leader starts to hum a tune. When she believes that the group has had sufficient time to hear the tune, she passes the tune to the neighbour on her left by gently squeezing his hand. At that moment, the group leader must stop humming, while her neighbour picks up the tune, hums it for a little while, and then passes it on to the neighbour on his left in the same way. Again, as in Game 56, *Letting energy flow*, with practice the tune could be made to flow backwards.

(58) Breathing in time

A volunteer stands somewhere in the room with his back to the rest of the group and begins, consciously, to breathe in and out. After a little while, a second player stands directly behind him and leans his chest against the back of the first player. Now both players try to breathe in and out in rhythm. A few moments later a third player joins them and leans against the back of the second player. Now all three players try to synchronise their breathing. In the course of time, more people can join in. The exercise would be particularly successful if the whole group managed to synchronise their breathing while leaning on each other.

(59) Parallel act

Two volunteers (A and B) go into the middle of the room. The group leader asks them to carry out some sort of everyday activity – for example, ordering a meal in a restaurant. The two volunteers now sit down at a table and the group leader or another player acts as a waiter and asks what the two customers would like to eat. They now have the difficult task of ordering a meal at the same time. They must leaf through the menu in a synchronised way, talk together (eg, 'I would like pasta bake'), and close the menu at exactly the same time. At which point do the two players manage to coordinate their actions exactly?

Materials: props for a restaurant table, menu

60 Scrambled syllables

A volunteer leaves the room. The other players divide into four groups of equal size and everyone thinks of a word that consists of at least four syllables. For example, if 'caterpillar' is chosen: Group 1 is assigned the first syllable, 'ca'; Group 2, the syllable 'ter'; Group 3 takes 'pil'; and Group 4 gets the syllable 'lar'. Now everybody walks around the room and each player calls out their assigned syllable. The group leader calls in the player who is standing outside the room. This player now needs to listen carefully and 'untangle' the syllables in order to determine which word the group has been practising.

Game variation

To vary the game slightly, ask the players to remain quiet after the syllables have been assigned to them. The player outside is called back to the room. Then, all at the same time, everybody calls out their syllable three times. It can be assumed that the player who has to guess the word will not be able to do this immediately. In that case, the group leader asks the other players to repeat the word. This time they can change the volume and tempo of the syllables, or even sing them along to a familiar tune.

61) Numbers in rhythm

The group makes a circle of chairs and the group leader models a three-part movement, just as in Game 36, *Nouns in rhythm*. She stamps her foot, slaps her hand on her thigh and then clicks her fingers. Initially the whole group carries out the exercise together. Everyone is then given a number to put on their chairs. The group goes through the movements again. While the players are slapping their thighs, the group leader calls out the number of her own chair (normally No 1). While everyone is clicking their fingers, the leader calls out another number, for example, No 6. This is the signal for the player in chair six to take over the group. The next time everyone slaps their thighs, he calls out his own number (No 6) and, when the finger clicking starts, he calls out another number (eg, No 8). Now the player in chair eight takes over. The procedure is repeated until everyone has had a go.

Anybody who reacts wrongly or misses the beat has to sit in the group leader's chair: everybody else has to move up a place and change their number to that of their new chair. The new number one once again begins the stamping, slapping and clicking.

62 Wink murder

All of the players spread out across the room and sit on the floor so they can see each other. The group leader hands out a playing card to each player. Everybody looks at their card without showing it to anybody else. The person who has the joker is the murderer. Now the game begins. As inconspicuously as possible, the murderer lets his eyes wander around the room. As soon as the murderer meets the eyes of another player, he winks at his victim. The person who has been winked at by the murderer is now dead. He reveals this to the other players by placing his card in front of him and calling, 'I am out!', but the murderer has to be very careful because the other players are out to expose him. Whoever thinks that he has observed the murderer winking at another person immediately calls out, 'I have a suspect!', and gives the name of the person he thinks is the murderer. If their suspicion is correct, a new round begins. If the suspect disputes that he is the murderer, the person who has made the false accusation has to place his card on the floor and is also out.

Materials: different playing cards, including a joker

63 Vampire game

Four players are selected and position themselves in the corners of the room. Their task is to ensure that, during the following game, the remaining players do not bump into a wall or into objects around the room (chairs, tables, etc). The other players close their eyes and walk around the room, but one player keeps his eyes open – he is the vampire looking for victims! The vampire pretends to suck his victims' blood by placing his hand on their necks. Each victim has to shout out once, and then he is out of the game. The other players walking around the room with their eyes closed have to try to sense where the vampire is; if they hear the shout of a victim close by, the vampire cannot be far away. The last player to be left 'alive' becomes the new vampire. The four players standing in the corners should also have a chance to play the game.

(64) Thief and guardian

The players sit in a circle, in the middle of which there is a piece of treasure (a randomly chosen object is fine). One player volunteers to be the 'thief' and leaves the room. A second player, still sitting in the circle, becomes the secret guardian of the treasure. The thief is called back in. He has to try to enter the circle to reach the treasure in the middle, then leave the circle by the same path. Without revealing his identity, the guardian tries to catch the thief while he is in the middle of the circle. However, the guardian is only allowed to move when the thief is actually touching the treasure. If the thief can get away from the circle with his loot without being touched by the guardian, the guardian is declared the thief and goes outside. Then a new guardian is chosen from the circle of players and the game begins again.

The particular challenge of this game is to try to tempt the guardian to drop his reserve, so that he reveals his identity before the thief actually touches the treasure. Make sure that the circle is made in such a way that the thief can gain free access at any point.

Materials: a random object

65 Dog and bone

Once again everybody sits in a circle on the floor. One player is blindfolded and sits in the centre. That player is the 'dog', guarding its bone with its ears pricked up. The group leader gives a silent sign to one of the players in the circle, at which point that player tries to approach the dog, steal the bone and take up his place in the circle again, without being noticed by the dog. If the dog hears a suspicious noise, it growls and points with its 'paw' in the direction from which it thinks the noise is coming. If the dog correctly identifies the bone thief, that person has to go back to their place in the circle, even if they already have the bone in their possession. In that case, a new thief is selected. If the dog has pointed in the wrong direction, the thief is allowed to press his luck further. If he manages to return to his original place with the bone, still unnoticed by the dog, a new dog is chosen.

Materials: a stick (for a bone)

66 Quiet footsteps

Everyone in the group lines up against a wall. A volunteer stands in front of the opposite wall, with his back towards the group. Without saying a word, the group now moves (if possible, in time) towards the player. As soon as the player hears any noise from the approaching group he lifts his hand. If that happens, the group has to move back to its initial position and try its luck once more. When the group is standing close enough to the volunteer for one member to put a hand on his shoulder, the round is finished, and a new volunteer takes his place.

(67) Who is calling the tune?

A volunteer leaves the room and the remaining players form an orchestra. A conductor is chosen and, while remaining in his place in the body of the orchestra, he has to play a selection of imaginary instruments, such as the piano, guitar, violin, bass, drums, cymbals, flute, trumpet, or mouth organ. Everybody else joins in, using the same instrument and accompanying their playing by singing a familiar song.

When the player outside is called back, the orchestra is in full swing, playing their instruments and singing along. At a silent signal from the conductor, they change instruments: they might start by playing the piano, then change to guitar and then to drums. The player who had been waiting outside now has to find out who is 'conducting' the other players. The players in the orchestra have to be careful not to look directly at the conductor, in order to make the task more difficult for the person who is guessing his identity.

68 A wall of people

A volunteer closes his eyes and stands in front of a wall facing into the room. The remaining players line up to form a wall of people at a distance from the volunteer. Then the volunteer starts to walk carefully, still with his eyes closed, towards the wall of people. While doing this, he has to assess the point at which he is standing directly in front of them: he must ensure that he stops in time to avoid colliding with the other players. The people who are part of the wall have to try to maintain complete silence, since any noise will alert the volunteer to their proximity.

Game variation

To vary the game, the volunteer could keep his eyes open while the wall of people is being formed. The volunteer has to estimate how many steps there are between him and the human wall; he needs to stop just short of the wall. Then he closes his eyes and takes that number of steps forward. The important thing is that each of his steps (including the last one) must be even – in other words, he must not slow down once he has started walking, or hesitate on his last step. It is interesting to observe how many people lose courage with their last step, so that it becomes smaller than the other steps they have taken.

Close enough to touch

Two people stand opposite each other at a reasonable distance and close their eyes. Then they begin to walk towards each other. Their task is to stop when they can just touch each other with outstretched hands.

 Piercing looks

The whole group, with the exception of one player, stands in a row. This player positions himself at a distance behind the row, facing the backs of the other players. Then he chooses one person from the group and stares at them intently. Every player in the row now has to try to sense if he is the object of the other player's penetrating stare. No talking is allowed during this exercise.

(71) Reciprocal touch

The players get together in pairs. One person in each pair closes his eyes. The other person now begins to describe the outline of his partner's body, with his hands approximately 10cm away from the body, avoiding any physical contact. The partner describing the body shape does not have to do this in sequence, from the top to the bottom. As in Game 70, *Piercing looks*, the important thing is that no sound is made, particularly by the person who is 'feeling' his partner's body. The person who has his eyes closed now tries to sense where his partner's hands are at any point in time. After a certain time, 'sensor' and 'feeler' swap roles.

72 Exchanging feelings

Two people stand opposite each other at least 5m apart, so that they are looking at one another. Each of them decides on a feeling, but the feelings chosen by the two partners must be opposites. For example, if player A decides on 'hatred', player B is assigned the feeling 'love'.

To begin with, the two players have to try building up that emotion inside themselves as much as possible. Once they have done this, the players wordlessly agree, through eye contact alone, to begin walking forward. They stop directly in front of each other. Then each of the two players tries to pass the feeling that he has built up inside himself to the other player and to take on his partner's feeling instead. (In the example above, player A would take on the feeling 'love', exchanging it for the 'hatred' of player B. From B's point of view, 'love' has been passed on to A and 'hatred' has been absorbed in its stead.) Only when both players are sure that the exchange has really been completed do they continue on their way.

Game variation
This game can be played with any emotion: joy and anger, hope and disappointment, happiness and bitterness, fear and courage, and so on. Subsequent reflection on the encounter by the rest of the group is important. What did the exchange of emotions seem like to the others? Should the two players have taken more time for their exchange?

(73) Trust pendulum

The players divide into groups of three. Two people stand opposite each other at a maximum of about 1.5 m apart. The third person stands between the two, with his face turned towards one of the players and his back towards the other. Then the player in the middle closes his eyes, tenses his body and carefully lets himself fall forward. The player standing in front of the falling person catches him by the shoulders. Then he carefully pushes the player in the opposite direction, so that the middle player now starts to fall backwards. The player behind the falling person catches him in the same manner and then pushes him back again. The game goes backwards and forwards several times. Then the players swap places, so everybody gets a chance to be the player in the middle.

After the exercise, the players should be given an opportunity to talk about their feelings during this game. How easy or difficult was it for each individual literally to 'let himself go', and to trust in the others to catch him?

74 Falling into the circle

The group forms a circle with a maximum of ten people. One player stands in the middle and closes his eyes. Then that player tenses his body and lets himself fall in any direction. The players surrounding him catch him and gently push him in a new direction. In this way, the person in the middle is pushed gently from one person to another. It is important that everybody in the circle is very careful as they handle the player in the middle.

(75) Blind lead

The group divides up into pairs. One player in each pair closes his eyes and extends one index finger in front of him. The second player now puts one of his own index fingers on top of his partner's and carefully begins to lead the 'blind' player through the room. While doing this, physical contact between the fingers has to be constant, as it is the only way for the person who is leading to indicate direction to the other player. It is crucial that the person leading is careful with the 'blind' player, continuously making sure that he does not bump into anything, including the wall. Again, no talking is allowed during this exercise.

Game variation

As an alternative, the partners do not make contact through their fingers, but instead the leading player directs the 'blind' player by gently tapping his back. A tap in the middle of the back means 'straight on', while a tap on the left or right shoulder means a change of direction to the left or right. After a little while, the roles are swapped. Afterwards, make sure the players talk about the exercise. Who enjoyed following blindly, and who felt uncomfortable?

(76) Camera

Two players, A and B, get together as a pair. Player B closes his eyes and player A places his hand on B's back, gently pushing B through the room. When A spots a particular 'snapshot' in the room (eg, spotlights on the ceiling), he gently directs B towards it and, when they are close enough to take a picture, carefully taps B on the head with his index finger. B then opens his eyes for a couple of seconds, saying 'click' loudly. Then B closes his eyes again and continues to let A lead him around the room. After taking a maximum of five 'pictures', A and B swap roles.

77 Leading and following

Two players, A and B, face each other at a distance that allows them to place the palms of their hands together. Now A, using palm pressure alone, pushes B through the room, and B lets this happen without fighting it. While doing this, A is clearly responsible for ensuring that B, who is moving backwards, does not bump into other pairs of players, objects in the room or the wall. After about two minutes, A and B swap roles.

Game variation

The players can then experiment: what happens when no one is leading, or both players want to lead at the same time? The group will quickly find that there is little or no movement in either scenario: both of the players are left standing still or, at the very least, they do not move very far. This situation can be applied to amateur dramatics: a scene between two or more people will only work if every player takes the lead on occasion, as well as letting the other players lead from time to time. In this way, everybody has the lead at some point, before passing it on to the other players.

(78) Humming vowels

All of the players lie on their backs and breathe slowly and evenly. After about two minutes, the group leader gives the instruction to hum a tune while breathing out. The players should try to hum using a particular vowel (eg, 'A'). This exercise is repeated about five times. Then the group leader gives the players a new vowel (E, I, O, U). These vowels, in turn, are hummed several times by everybody. Afterwards, the group can discuss which sound was the easiest to breathe out and which caused the most difficulties.

Imagination & Improvisation

Imagination and the art of improvisation both play a special role in amateur dramatics. Neither one is about setting limits, but going beyond them and pushing the boundaries. Both provide opportunities for people to create their own experience and to find out more about themselves. As a result, many people discover new abilities and aspects of themselves that they did not know existed. Improvisation in particular can test the way in which individuals deal with unpredictable situations, sometimes transforming them into positive learning experiences. In the process, people have stretched themselves further than they dreamed possible.

The following games will enable everybody to learn to allow the natural progression of their own emotions. The general motto is: 'Aim high!'

79 Magical air

The group stands in a circle. The first player draws an imaginary object (eg, a guitar) in the 'magical' air of the room. He then uses the object to act out a scenario. Using the guitar, for example, he may strum like a rock star. Afterwards, using his hands, he reshapes the object into a little ball of magic air and passes this on to his neighbour. Now it is the next player's turn to shape another object and to play with it. Depending on the size of the group, this game can be played over several rounds.

80 Mirror, mirror, on the wall

Players A and B stand opposite each other. Player B represents A's mirror image. Player A performs a sequence of movements, perhaps stretching his arms up in the air, turning his head to one side, sticking out his tongue, and alternating these movements with pushing the palms of his hands further and further out to his sides. Player B now has to copy these movements as exactly as possible, with the minimum lapse of time after their demonstration. The players are not allowed to talk. After two minutes or so, B takes the lead, and A becomes his mirror image.

Game variation

To vary the game, instead of swapping roles after a given time, either partner might try to take over the lead or hand it over to the other person, still without talking to each other. In this way, everyone can be both the real person and the mirror image, all in the space of a few seconds.

(81) Yes and no

Two volunteers stand in the middle of the room. Player A takes up an open body posture, walks towards B and says loudly and clearly, 'Yes!' While doing this, A can try to touch B. Player B, on the other hand, assumes a hostile body posture, turns away from A and says loudly and determinedly 'No!' During the course of the game, A repeatedly tries to get closer to B, by continuing to say 'Yes!' B, in turn, continues to reject A and says 'No!' in a decisive manner. Afterwards, the roles are swapped, and then two more people form a pair and repeat the exercise, while the rest of the group watches. Once everybody has had a turn, the players should use discussion to explore which role was the most difficult.

From experience, it seems that most people find the open 'yes' approach more difficult. Many people appear to find it easier to say 'no' and reject someone.

82 Word and movement

The players sit together on the floor in a circle. The first player says a word, then makes a movement that has no connection with the word spoken. For example, player A might say 'biro', and stick out his tongue. The player to his left (player B) repeats both the word and the movement, and then adds his own. For example, he might say 'houseboat', and point to his watch. The player to his left (player C) carries on, first repeating player A's word and movement, then player B's, before adding his own. He might say, for example, 'potato', and close his eyes.

Where are the first difficulties in repeating words and movements going to occur? Or is the group going to manage to get through the round without stumbling?

83 Treasure hunt

This game is a great exercise for reducing inhibitions, especially when addressing total strangers. *Treasure hunt* is best played during the course of a meeting, a rehearsal or a seminar that is taking place in a strange, rather than a familiar, environment (eg, a different town). The players get together in pairs, arm themselves with pen and paper and are given one object per pair. Each group could receive either the same object or different ones. Items such as toy cars, pebbles, pencils, and so on, are suitable.

Now the game moves outside onto the street. There, each group tries to engage a passer-by in conversation and then convince this person to agree to a swap. During the course of the exchange, each pair gives the object that they have been given to the passer-by. The passer-by has to give them any other object that he may be carrying on his person at the time: a (clean!) paper hanky, a pen, a business card, a sweet, and so on. The only condition is that the group members are not allowed to take money as part of the exchange. They then move on to the next passer-by with their new object and aim for another exchange. One member of each pair records the individual exchanges in writing. Each group should be honest while doing this and not invent any fictitious exchanges. After a previously agreed period of time (about one hour), all of the players meet up again.

The final stage is not about determining which group can boast the most exchanges in order to determine a winner. Rather, it is much more important and interesting if all the players tell each other of their impressions and the experiences they had during the game. The players should also exchange their insights on the ease or difficulty with which individual players were able to approach total strangers and make their requests. Did they lose some of their inhibitions during the course of the game?

Materials: a selection of small objects, paper, pens

84 Rain dance

The players can sit on the floor or stand, whichever they prefer. One person begins the game by beating out a particular rhythm (eg, 3/4 time), using his hands or feet. The second person takes over with a new rhythm by clapping a different pattern or time signature. One after the other, each player contributes to this rhythm round in their own individual way. It does not matter whether players drum against the floor, the wall, or even their own bodies. Anyone can accompany his own beat with other noises at regular intervals if he wishes – for example, hissing, whistling, humming, and so on. Regardless of what kind of rhythm and what sort of noise the individual players prefer, it always sounds impressive when a large group 'makes music' in this way. Players can throw themselves into the activity so much that the whole 'ceremony' begins to resemble a kind of conjuration – hence the name 'rain dance'.

Materials: small drums (if available), large tin cans and anything that can be used to make a percussive sound

85 Human machine

A volunteer starts the game by standing in the middle of the room and performing an action he has chosen to resemble a mechanical process. For example, the player may kneel on the floor while banging his fist on it at regular intervals as if he was knocking something into the ground. After a short while, another player joins him. He makes physical contact with the first player, eg, by leaning on his back. Then the second player also performs a repetitive mechanical movement, for example bringing his hands together in front of his chest over and over again. The game continues in the same way: one by one new players join, make physical contact with the previous player and choose a movement until all of the group members are united in the workings of this 'machine'. If they wish, the players can also accompany their movement with a noise, such as loud groaning, whistling or grinding. Finally the machine's movements become faster and faster, and the noises louder and louder, until the whole game peaks in massive chaos, and the machine 'explodes' with a loud bang. The group should choose this point in time without talking to each other, but simply by following a joint impulse.

86 Popping the corks

The players sit in two rows facing each other. Each player holds a cork between his front teeth. The player on the far right of one row begins the game by shouting out some sort of mild insult at the person opposite (eg, 'twit!'), while still trying to hold the cork in his mouth. The person addressed now turns to the player sitting to the left of the player opposite and insults this player in turn ('idiot!'). That person, again, now turns to the person directly opposite and insults them ('dumbo!'). Once the game has reached the end of both rows, the insults should travel back in reverse, so that the person who opened the game also gets insulted once. The kind of insults allowed should be agreed at the beginning of the game to ensure that no one has his feelings hurt. This game is simply about loosening up, and seeing who can manage to hold on to their cork.

Materials: lots of corks

87) What might you be ...?

Considering one person at a time, the group thinks about which objects individual group members might be, if they were not people. They might be, for example, cars (sports cars, estate cars, jeeps); colours (red, blue, green); plays (comedy, drama, musical); stretches of water (a still ocean, a raging river); houses (a cottage, a castle, a farm); seasons (spring, summer, autumn, winter); animals or birds (lion, mouse, peacock); countries (Spain, Norway); or one of the elements (earth, water, fire, air).

Can the individual discussed identify with the suggestions of the group? If so, why? If not, why not? And is there another object which, in his opinion, would be more appropriate? This game can also be played when group members do not yet know each other very well. In fact this might be a particularly interesting stage for each person to discover the impression the others have gained of him in a short space of time.

88) Celebrities on the couch

Two volunteer players leave the room. The rest of the group agrees which two celebrities or well-known characters the two should represent. These could be real or fictional figures, celebrities that are alive or dead (eg, Michael Jackson or Marilyn Monroe). When the two volunteers return to the room they take a seat on the 'celebrity couch' (use a couple of chairs). As they do not have a clue who they now are, they have to discover their identity by listening to and interpreting the other players' questions and comments. Michael Jackson, for example, could be asked, 'Is your nose all right?' Marilyn Monroe might receive the compliment, 'How do you manage to look so good after you have been dead for decades?' The two celebrities obviously have to try to give quick-witted answers, even though they do not have any idea of their own identities. This game guarantees fun for both sides, if the questions are reasonably original and do not make it too easy for the two celebrities to guess their identities.

89 Press conference

Two people volunteer to be celebrities. In contrast to Game 88, *Celebrities on the couch*, these people already know which famous characters they are representing (eg, Madonna and Michael Schumacher). They sit down at a table and face the group, which proceeds to cross-examine them about their celebrity lives. The group may question the two celebrities in as much detail as they like, including questions about the private lives of the two stars (eg, whether or not the two have ever had an affair, whether Madonna would consider having a go as a racing driver, or if Schumacher is envisaging a career as a pop star). The audience is also allowed to interrupt the two from time to time (don't overdo it!). Afterwards, two new celebrities volunteer themselves.

(90) Change of scenery

Two volunteers start to act out an everyday scene for the rest of the group: for example, a couple are on their way to the theatre and get involved in a serious argument. After a minute or so, one of the group members watching claps his hands. The two volunteer actors have to freeze immediately when they hear the clap. The person who has clapped determines which of the two actors has to leave the stage. Then the 'clapper' takes over the role of the person who has left, and the drama continues, this time with a different starting point. The new beginning is determined by the new actor, and it must take place in a totally different situation from the previous one. For example, the two characters are not a married couple any more, but a buyer and sales assistant in an expensive boutique. After a minute or so, a clap from the audience signals the same exchange of roles as previously. The scene is once again transferred to a different context and then continued. This exercise lasts long enough for each player to have at least one turn at being an actor.

91) Sales talk

The group leader asks everyone to choose one object in the room or to bring an object to the meeting. The object could be anything: for example, a pen, a glass, a CD, and so on. When everybody has their chosen object, the leader tells them that the players now have to take it in turn to extol their objects as the latest new sensations. Each player has to try to convince the other players that they are going to miss out if they do not possess such an object. Objects can be offered for the purpose intended, or they could be offered for a different purpose – for example, a bottle could be 'sold' as a particularly special bottle, or as a kind of tool. The game becomes even more interesting if the audience is allowed to ask the seller questions about the product concerned.

Materials: any objects

92 Story game

Using one piece of paper for each word, the group leader writes down words that can be linked into a story or fairy tale (fairy, magician, elf, boy, girl, giant, hut, forest, mountain, river, winter). Alternatively, the group leader could choose a selection of random words. Now the group sits together and each player picks one or several pieces of paper. Then the first player begins to tell his story, talking for about one minute. During this time, he has to incorporate the words on his pieces of paper. After one minute, his neighbour has to continue the story. He, too, has one minute, and he, too – as well as all of the subsequent players – has to knit together the words on the pieces of paper, regardless of whether, at first sight, the words fit into the narrative or not. Anybody who misses out a word, or hesitates for too long, is out.

Game variation

This exercise can also be played as a group game. In that case, two (or more) teams are formed and each team in turn has to tell the story, until every player has had a turn. Points are deducted for every word left out and for hesitation.

Materials: paper, pens

93 Pig-plague

The group leader writes down on a piece of paper an uncommon noun or an invented compound noun (eg, pig-plague) for each player. Each player picks a piece of paper and reads his word without showing it to anybody else. Then the group leader tells a story, or reads from a book or newspaper. The leader stops suddenly in mid flow. The players now have to continue the story, using their imagination. While doing this, they must incorporate the word on their piece of paper into the story, without making it stand out.

The story is passed from storyteller to storyteller after about a minute (the group should decide on the order in advance). The players have to listen carefully to determine which word each player has incorporated into the story. It is a good idea if players record their suspicions on a separate piece of paper. Comparisons are made at the end of the round. Who has kept their face straight and incorporated their word into the story without anybody noticing? Who was found out? How?

Materials: paper, pens

94 Emotional fields

The group leader places four flat cardboard squares of equal size next to each other on the floor. Each of these 'fields' is now assigned a particular emotion. For example: Field A may represent anger; Field B, joy; Field C, fear; and Field D, grief. One after the other, each player walks slowly over the emotional fields as the other players watch. Depending on the field on which a player stands at the time, he has to try to express that feeling to the observers. Afterwards the players should discuss the feeling which was easiest to represent and which was the most difficult. Which person was particularly convincing in their expression of a particular feeling?

Materials: four cardboard squares of equal size

95 Mime chain

Depending on the size of the group, between three and five players are sent outside. The rest of the group thinks of a situation for a particular person who has remained in the room to mime (eg, washing an elephant). The chosen person positions himself in the middle of the room, and the first of the players outside is asked to come back into the room. The player in the middle of the room now acts out the agreed mime. The player who has returned to the room has to try to remember all of his movements as precisely as possible.

Once the player in the middle has finished his mime, the player who has been studying him positions himself in the middle of the room. Then the next person is called back into the room and has to pay close attention to the player in the middle as he tries to repeat the previous mime as accurately as possible. Then the next person is called back into the room and the observer once again becomes the mime artist.

At the end, the players who have been outside the room have to try to guess what action the mime was supposed to represent. Other mimes for performance might include mending a flat tyre; changing a baby's nappy; and an aeroplane landing.

96 Emotional mime

The players form two groups, A and B. Each group selects an emotion without telling the other group what it is. Then group A begins to mime its emotion (eg, loneliness, grief, anger, fear, happiness, hope) as a tableau – a posed picture of everyone in the group, standing motionless. Group B carefully studies the tableau and tries to guess the emotion portrayed. Once the emotion has been guessed, group A should remain in its tableau for a moment, so that, if necessary, group B can make changes which might express more clearly the emotion concerned: for example, group B could change the body postures of some of the members of group A. Then group B has to mime an emotion, group A has to guess it and, if they wish, they are allowed to 'correct' the picture created by group B.

97 Modelling a mime

The group leader names a particular emotion for the players to represent (eg, grief). Then the group divides up into pairs. Player A stands with his legs slightly apart and lets his arms and head droop forward. Player B has to change A's body posture in such a way that A will be expressing the named emotion: B is allowed to change the position of A's upper and lower body. As long as it feels comfortable, A just lets this happen to him. At the end, the players who have been the sculptors walk from 'statue' to 'statue' and decide who has best managed to express a particular emotion. Then the partners swap roles.

98 Comedy mime

The players split into different groups of at least three people per group. The group leader hands out a piece of paper to each group. On the piece of paper there is a brief description of a funny situation which the group now has to act out for the other players in any way they like: the challenge is that the scenarios must be portrayed through mime, without using words. Suitable scenarios include:

◆ Several people, including a woman in the late stages of pregnancy, meet for coffee and a gossip. Just as the gossip is beginning to flow, the pregnant woman goes into labour.

◆ A group of people is waiting at the bus stop. One after another, they suddenly change into animals (monkey, lion, crow, snake, and so on). How are they behaving now?

◆ A couple is standing at the altar. Just as the ceremony is about to begin, the groom realises that his best man has forgotten the rings. What now?

◆ Three actors are on a stage acting out a play. The fourth actor is lying next to the stage asleep. His cue comes, but, of course, he misses it. The other actors repeat the scene, the cue once again fails, and the prompter does not know what to do next. How does this chaos end?

It will be interesting to find out what individual groups think of to complete the scenes. It will also be interesting to see whether the audience recognises the scenes as clearly as the actors intended.

99 Conflict mime

This variation on Game 98, *Comedy mime*, also requires the players to divide into groups of at least three people. The group leader gives each group a critical situation which they then have to mime, and everyone present should be aware of the crisis being portrayed. Situations to mime include:

◆ Group A is on a ship that is threatening to sink.
◆ Group B is stuck in a lift.
◆ Group C has to get itself to safety during a raging storm.
◆ Group D is trapped in a cave.

While one group is acting, the others have to observe them carefully: in which way does each group manage to solve the given conflict? Which person is taking the lead? Which people are happy to be led, or are the relationships more evenly balanced? Who is miming a realistic response to the crisis?

Materials: props necessary for the scenes

100 Scene exit (1)

The players form groups of between two and four people. Each group chooses one person to be their 'commentator'. Then each group acts out a scene chosen by the commentator, which should be based on his own experience. These could be funny or serious situations, for example a first meeting with a girl or boyfriend that went slightly wrong, or an unsuccessful job interview. The commentator also performs in the play. However, at times of his own choosing, he has to step out of the play and address the audience while the remaining players freeze their actions. The commentator then explains to the audience how he felt at that precise moment in the real situation. Subsequently, he rejoins the scene and the action continues. The commentator should not break out of the scene more than three or four times.

After all of the groups have offered a scene, the whole group can discuss the scenarios, perhaps raising the following points: who has experienced a similar situation? Did the feelings of the commentator correspond to the feelings that others have experienced in parallel situations? Who was best able to communicate their feelings to the audience?

Materials: props necessary for different scenarios

(101) Picture stories

Before the beginning of the meeting, the group leader prepares an assortment of pictures from newspapers and magazines – advertisements are particularly suitable for this game. The pictures should represent people in a variety of situations. The players divide into groups of equal size, ideally three to six people per group. Each group is now given a minimum of three and a maximum of five pictures and has to link the pictures together to form a continuous story. The story should then be acted out by the respective group as a short scene, lasting no longer than ten minutes. While they are acting, the players have to ensure that they assume exactly the same positions and postures as the people in their pictures in order to depict the situations accurately. Afterwards, the group as a whole should reflect on which group was best at incorporating their pictures into a scene and which group might have slightly missed the topic, or failed to make the situations clear enough.

> **Materials:** pictures from newspapers and magazines, any necessary props

102 Incorporating body postures into a scene (1)

A group of about five people spreads out across the room. Each player tries out three different body postures, holding each posture for about one minute. These body postures could involve standing, sitting or lying positions. Once the players have practised their three positions they act out a scene (which should last no longer than five minutes) whose content has been roughly outlined by the group leader, detailing location, sequence of events, short character descriptions, etc. The players have to incorporate the three body postures from the first part of this exercise into the dramatised scene. The audience, formed from the rest of the group, is requested to observe the players carefully and to give feedback at the end. Were the body postures clearly recognisable? Were they suited to the sequence of events, or the represented figure? If something was successful, why was this? If unsuccessful, why so?

Messages in gibberish

The players get together in pairs. Player A in each pair is handed a piece of paper by the group leader, which must not be shown to his partner. The piece of paper carries a message that player A has to communicate to player B. To complicate the task, player A is only allowed to talk gibberish consisting of a mishmash of consonants and vowels sounds (eg, 'Brrrraaaaaknnnnhussssilutgkiion'). Player B, for his part, has to try to decode the message. Is it possible for the players to communicate a message simply by their actions?

The players could act out these scenarios:

◆ A tries to convince B to fetch some coffee for him.
◆ A wants to swap wallets with B.
◆ A asks B where the toilets are.
◆ A wants to tell B that he has lost his contact lenses.

Game variation

Instead of using gibberish, the players could express their messages using a numeric code.

104 Finding excuses

The players get together in pairs and the group leader hands out a written description of a particular scenario to player A in each pair. Player B is not allowed to see this description. The leader tells player B and the audience where the scene takes place and how it starts, for example, 'This scene takes place at a border crossing. A is the customs officer, while B wants to get across the border'. The secret ingredient to this game is that there is a crucial piece of information about the scene on A's piece of paper that will put B into an embarrassing situation. For example, player A's piece of paper describes the entire scenario: 'This scene is taking place at a border crossing. You are the customs officer. Your player A wants to cross the border. You search his luggage and discover contraband'.

Players A and B then begin to act out their scene. Player A asks player B to show him his luggage and, after searching his bags, he suddenly holds up one item, asking, 'Why have you got alcohol in your luggage?' Player B needs to come up with an excuse. How will he save himself? The players could also try these scenarios:

◆ A and B meet in the pub. Player A explains that their joint ticket has won the lottery and wants to know where the lottery ticket is. Regardless of what B shows him, A tells him that this is not the lottery ticket. How is B going to talk himself out of this one?

◆ A is a teacher at a drama school. B presents himself as an applicant for a scholarship. A requests that B acts out any part of his choice. B now has to make something up. However, after a very short time, A interrupts the scene and asks B to act out another part. But the new scene is also interrupted quickly, and B is requested to act out something else. Will B finally manage to convince A to give him the scholarship?

Materials: props necessary for the scenes

(105) Self-assertion game

The players form groups consisting of four to five people. Each group is given a scene to act out for the others in turn. The aim is for the individual players to put themselves over as well as possible – in other words really to assert themselves. At the end of each scene, the whole group should discuss which player was best able to assert himself, and how he did this. Who found it more difficult?

(106) Charades

The players divide into two groups and compete with each other in a game of charades. The group leader prepares a number of pieces of paper on which are written familiar terms, well-known sayings, or the names of famous people. The first player from group A goes up to the leader who shows him a piece of paper. Then A begins to mime whatever is on the paper for his group. If the group guesses the word within a given time (eg, one minute), it is awarded one point. Then it is the turn of the other group to mime something. The game should continue until each player has had at least one turn at miming. Items to be guessed could include famous people: singers such as Elvis Presley; actors such as Julia Roberts; and politicians such as Tony Blair. Other things to mime include sayings such as 'The early bird catches the worm', TV soaps (eg, 'Eastenders'), films (eg, 'Terminator'), jobs (eg, midwife), compound words (eg, shoelace), and embarrassing situations (eg, being caught having an affair). The list of possibilities is endless, and the group awarded the most points wins the game.

Materials: paper, pens

Miming situations

The players form groups of from two to five people. Each group now acts out a given scene for the rest, without using words. This scene could be about anything, for example: a couple who have had a big argument the night before are sitting at the breakfast table the next morning, still in a bad mood; a blind person wakes up during the night when he hears a noise; a group of people get stuck in an elevator; and so on.

The audience has to try to guess the situation which is being mimed. After a scene has been acted out, the players should immediately reflect on it together. Was the situation portrayed clearly? If it was, how was this achieved? If it wasn't, why did it fail? Which feelings were predominantly portrayed during the scene? What sort of atmosphere did the whole scene have?

Then it is the next group's turn to mime another situation.

(108) Beginnings and endings

The players form groups of two or more people. The group leader provides a scenario for each group to act out after the group has had some time to discuss it – however, she has already decided what the beginning and the ending of the scene are to be and tells everyone before they start. So, in the course of the game, each group has to think about acting their way through from a given beginning to a given ending. Scenarios to try include:

◆ *Beginning*: several patients are sitting in a dentist's or psychiatrist's waiting room.
   End: all have fled, for whatever reason.
◆ *Beginning*: two (married) couples who have fallen out with each other meet in court.
   End: The parties make up.
◆ *Beginning*: a club meets for its AGM. The chairman opens the meeting.
   End: At the end of the meeting, to his surprise, the chairman has been voted out and someone else is sitting in his place.

Materials: props necessary for the scenes

109 Discussing and role-playing different scenarios

A volunteer sits on a chair at the edge of the room – she is the narrator. A group made up of three to five players are the actors, all of whom are given a role name, if not an actual character. The remaining players watch the scene that follows.

The narrator begins to tell a story, sentence by sentence, which is acted out by the selected group: 'One evening, four friends meet at the pub'. The actors meet in the middle of the room, greet each other and sit on chairs in a circle. The narrator continues: 'Hannah tells everybody that she was involved in a car accident yesterday'. The actress previously chosen to play Hannah now tells the rest of the group, in her own words, how the accident happened. The narrator can determine the course of the story, since he is the director. Anything could happen, for example one of the actors might spill his beer; a fire could break out in the pub; there could be a flood; and so on.

The situations can be comic, or they could be more serious. The scene should last no longer than ten minutes and should have a recognisable ending. After the scene has been discussed, the game starts again from the beginning, with a new volunteer telling another story, acted out by a new group of actors.

Materials: props necessary for the scenes

(110) Imaginary world

Get the group to form smaller groups of four or five people. Each group is assigned a different opening situation by the group leader, which it then has to develop into a complete scene. The challenge lies in the dramatic turn which the scene must take after it has been running for a couple of minutes, following the instructions of the group leader who will steer it towards a surreal, imaginary world. The actors now have to work out how to cope with this new situation. Here are some examples:

◆ A few people are travelling together in the same railway carriage. They talk animatedly about the state of the world. Then the group leader steps in to instruct them: 'The train stops at a station and you get out. The train drives off and, all of a sudden, you realise that there is nothing all around you: no houses, no trees, no shrubs, no earth, no sky. There is not the tiniest sign of the material world'. How are the players going to cope in this limbo?

◆ A couple is sitting in front of the television. They are having an animated discussion and are not paying much attention to the film being shown (which is being performed by some of the actors in the group). Then the group leader calls out: 'The characters on the screen now demand that the couple pays more attention to the film!' Where will this surreal situation end?

◆ Four people carry out a given job: person A kneads an imaginary object and passes it on to B, B works the object in a different manner and then passes it to C, C works the object in yet another way, before passing it on to D. The group continues moving like a conveyor belt for about one minute. Then the leader calls out: 'You are all organs of the human body: specifically, you are the stomach, the small and large intestines and the liver. Continue working, but have a conversation with each other as well'. What might the organs talk about while doing their jobs?

◆ A group of people meets at a friend's house to go to the cinema. Everyone puts on his coat and the house owner opens the door. Just as he is about to step outside, the group leader calls out: 'You realise that the house is in the middle of a football field. Arsenal are about to play Manchester United!' How are the people involved going to react? Can they see the humour in this situation? Or are they going to panic?

◆ A group of people is walking through the zoo and looking at the animals. After a while, the group leader calls out: 'You are beginning to notice that it is not the animals, but you, who are in the cages – you are being studied by the animals!'

The aim of the game is for actors to carry on playing their roles, in spite of the awkward situations in which they find themselves.

> **Materials:** props necessary for the scenes

(111) Opera – Western – horror movie

At the beginning of the game, the group leader chooses several random sentences, perhaps from a daily newspaper. The group leader writes each sentence on a different piece of paper. Then the players are divided into a total of five groups, with at least four people in each. The groups are given three to five pieces of paper, on which are written the sentences. Now every group has to act out some kind of scene for the other players, but there are three rules:

1 Each group has to incorporate their assigned sentences into their scene.
2 Lots are drawn to determine the dramatic style that the individual groups will use to act out their scene: one group will have to act out their scene as an opera; another, as a ballet; the third group, as a horror film; the fourth, as a Western; and the last group has to put on a tragedy.
3 They must act according to the style assigned to them. In opera, dialogues are sung, not spoken, but the singing skills of the individuals involved are of no significance during this game. Ballet requires the actors to dance. In a horror film, the actors have to try to create a terrifying and gruesome atmosphere. A Western must include (imaginary) horses, guns and cowboys. Finally, the main element of a tragedy is that at least one character has to die.

Which group is going to incorporate its random sentences in the most original way?

Game variation
As an additional task, each group can be given specific props to build into the action.

> **Materials:** newspaper, paper, pen, props necessary for the scenes

(112) A big can of beans

Two volunteers are given a scene to play by the group leader. The volunteers have to follow the exact dialogue given to them. Player A is a sales assistant in a grocery store and player B is the customer. B enters the shop and says, 'Hello. I would like a big can of beans, please!' A takes an imaginary can of beans from an imaginary shelf and hands it to B with the words, 'Here you are. That's £1 [or equivalent amount in relevant currency], please'. B gives A the imaginary money and says, 'There you are'. A takes the money and says 'Thank you'. Then B leaves the shop and the scene is finished.

Now the actual game begins. A and B have to play the scene again several times, making a significant change each time. The first time, each sentence has to be said as loudly as possible: during this run, the dialogue between A and B will obviously become a huge shouting match. Then both players are asked to play the scene in slow motion: this means that both their movements and speech have to be dragged out, as if they were talking and moving through treacle. Finally, the scene is acted out in a rush, with their movements and speech speeded up as much as possible.

Game variations

A new scene is chosen, perhaps taking place in a bank this time. Player A is the bank clerk and player B wants to get out some money. The dialogue is changed accordingly.

You can play as many variations as you like, which would enable different players to have a turn. This exercise is a good way of demonstrating how drastically a scene can be changed, even though the dialogue stays exactly the same.

Changing details

Two volunteers act out a given scene together. Players A and B cuddle up to each other on a 'sofa' (use two chairs pushed together), then begin the dialogue, adhering to it word for word:

A: Is something the matter?
B: Hmmm?
A: Is something wrong?
B: With what?
A: With you.
B: Why? What did I say?
A: You haven't said anything.
B: Well, there you go!

Then they act out the scene again. However, in contrast to Game 112, *A big can of beans*, it is not the pace or the intonation that should be changed for the second run, but only the positions of the two players. This time, A sits at a table and stares straight ahead, while B stands with his face turned to the wall and looks out of an imaginary window, so that both players have neither physical nor visual contact as they repeat the dialogue. Afterwards, the rest of the group, who are watching the scene, have to say how the scene changed when the actors repositioned themselves. Compared to the first run, did a different mood come across the second time? For the third run, A sits at the table again and stares straight ahead, while B stands behind A holding a knife. Then both players repeat the dialogue. What changes this time, when a prop is incorporated into the scene?

After renewed reflection within the group, two new volunteers are selected to act out another dialogue, following the same sequence of runs as used for the previous scene.

Materials: props as required

(114) Developing characters (1)

At the beginning of the game the group leader puts a selection of different hats in the middle of the room. There have to be at least as many hats as there are players. At the group leader's signal, all of the players choose a hat and put it on. The group leader then tells everyone to walk around the room. Now each player has to think of a character who would suit the hat they are currently wearing, make up a special walk for that character, and use it to move around the room. Then the group leader asks everyone, without stopping, to create a more detailed mental image of the character, one befitting the hat and the walk. The players need to think about the following details: the person's name, his age, where he lives, whether he has a job and, if so, what it is; his appearance, whether or not he has a disability; his marital status; and his most noticeable character trait. The seminar leader should allow at least a quarter of an hour for this part of the exercise. Then all of the players finish walking and sit down.

One at a time, players are requested to introduce themselves in the role of their character: they have to describe themselves, their environment, their family, and so on. The other players are allowed to ask questions about the imaginary character, and the player who has invented him must reply in detail. While doing this, the player should remain in character.

Once everybody has introduced themselves and the group has formed a picture of the different characters, the players get together in pairs. The pairs take it in turns to act out short scenes, still in character. Meanwhile, the rest of the group has to assess how well the two are really playing their roles. How is the scene introduced and how does it develop? A clear ending is important. There is one simple rule for each scene: the two people meeting must act as if they have never met each other before. Afterwards, the group can debate the following questions: which encounter was the most interesting? Why? Was it due to one individual or to the combination of the two characters that a scene was particularly funny, tragic or intense?

Materials: large number of different hats

(115) Shifting walls

Each player stands facing the wall. The distance from player to wall should be such that the players have to stretch out their arms to place their palms flat on it. At the group leader's signal, the players push against the wall with all their body weight, as if they are trying to shift it. While doing this, each player could imagine that the wall is a feeling, a situation, an object, or even a person that he is trying to ban from his life. The players could shout out sounds, words or whole sentences which come to mind during the exercise. When an individual comes to the point where he has used up all his energy, he should sit with his back to the wall, breathing slowly and evenly. During this phase of the exercise, everybody can once more express the feelings that they experienced while trying to shift the wall. This game is good for decreasing aggression and inhibitions.

(116) One sentence and three themes

Groups of between three and five people are formed. Each group chooses a line from a familiar children's song or a nursery rhyme. Then they work out a scene, which contains at least three varied themes, such as love, money and death. The difficulty is that the players are only allowed to use their chosen sentence to convey the situation, the feelings and the personalities of the characters to their audience; apart from this one sentence, no other verbal expression is allowed.

Once all of the groups have acted out their scenes, the whole group holds a discussion. Did everyone manage to convey clearly the content of the scene using only one sentence? If they did manage it, how was this done? If not, why didn't it work?

117 Act physical

Six players at a time work together as a team. Three of them form group A, while the others are in group B. Group A starts a trivial conversation about any topic, such as the weather. All of the players are required to keep their hands on one part of their bodies at all times (eg, on their knees, on their stomachs, on their chins, and so on). They are not allowed to remove their hands from their bodies for even one second. Then group B debates the same topic. These players are not allowed to have their hands on their bodies at any time during the conversation, instead they have to gesticulate

Game variation

Vary this game by getting the six players from groups A and B to pretend they have a physical feature which keeps coming up during the conversation – for example, a nervous eye twitch, a lisp, a shoulder twitch, a stiff neck, a permanent itch, toothache, sweaty hands, and so on. This exercise quickly demonstrates how a trivial text can become funny if certain body postures are incorporated.

Closing Exercises

A good finish is just as important as a successful beginning for any workshop or seminar. Nothing is more unsatisfactory than seeing players simply walk away from each other, without reflection, after an intensive period of work. Everyone should be given the opportunity to end their time together quietly, without rushing. During such closing rounds the players can reflect on their experiences and discoveries one last time – if they wish, by involving the group. The aim of these activities is that all of the players should go home feeling good, taking with them specific impressions and memories. Where the exercises involve massage, take time to ensure that each person has the opportunity to choose a partner he trusts and in whom he feels confident.

EXERCISES FOLLOWING AN INTENSE PERIOD OF WORK
Exercises 130–35 are less suited to closing a rehearsal, but are good for concluding a longer or more intense period of work, such as a seminar or workshop.

(118) Mutual relaxation

The group splits up into pairs. Player A sits in a comfortable position on a chair, closes his eyes and lets his entire body relax, with arms, legs and head hanging as loosely as possible. Player B starts, very gently, to massage A's body from head to toe, assessing where A is still tense and therefore not yet sufficiently relaxed. If B finds any such places, it is his job to loosen these up, moving them very carefully (eg, lifting and lowering the arms) in order to help A relax. B has to be extremely sensitive while doing this, first, in order to identify correctly these tense areas and, second, in order to maintain A's trust, since, by the act of closing his eyes, A has literally given himself over into B's hands. This exercise is only finished when B has helped free his partner from all his tensions. As a last act, B gently strokes A's back. This is the signal to swap roles. A slowly opens his eyes and lets the relaxation take effect for a little longer. Then B sits down on the chair and closes his eyes, allowing himself to be relaxed by A in the same way.

(119) Pummel massage

Two people of approximately the same body size pair up to give each other a pummel massage. Player A stands his feet hip-width apart on the floor and lets his upper body flop forward. B stands behind A and gently pummels A's body up and down with flattened hands, taking care around the area of the spine. A keeps his mouth open and makes a humming sound (the vowel sounds, 'Aaaaa' or 'Oooooo', are most effective) while breathing out. To finish the massage, B briskly strokes A's back, legs and arms with flattened hands. Then A and B change roles.

120 Whole-body massage

The group divides into pairs. Player A lies on his stomach and closes his eyes. B kneels down next to A and gently begins to massage his partner, starting with the shoulder areas, continuing with the arms and then slowly working down across A's back. The upper and lower thighs, as well the feet, will particularly benefit from this massage. It is important that B works gently and slowly, so that A can enjoy the massage. To finish, B could again gently stroke A's back, or even the entire length of his body. Once A has enjoyed the after-effects of the exercise for a few moments, both partners swap roles.

(121) Brush massage

Two group members can massage each other using a brush (most suitable are make-up brushes, with heads approximately 5cm long). Individuals can decide for themselves whether they prefer to lie on their backs or on their stomachs. Instead of massaging partner A's body with his hands, B carefully brushes A's body.

Materials: several (make-up) brushes

(122) Weather massage

The players get together in groups of five. One person lies on his stomach and closes his eyes. The others kneel down around that person and begin their 'weather massage'. First, light rain falls: during this phase, the four kneeling people gently drum their fingers on the back of the person lying down. After a little while, the rain becomes heavier: accordingly, their fingers begin to drum more firmly. Eventually, there is a real cloudburst: the fingers become very insistent as they drum. Then a strong wind picks up: during this phase, the four kneeling players rock the person lying down backwards and forwards, gently at first, then more strongly. The sound of the wind blowing is created by the four masseurs, as is the thunder that begins to sound. Next, the masseurs continue 'raining' their fingers down on their friend's back: the rain is still strong, but after a while it lets up, little by little, until it finally stops. Now comes the last phase of the exercise: the sun makes an appearance. To create this effect, the masseurs carefully place their palms on their friend's back as well as his upper and lower thighs: he now feels and soaks up the warmth of the sun through their hands. Afterwards, the players swap roles until eventually every person in the group has had a chance to enjoy a weather massage.

(123) Pizza toppings

This game is a variation on Game 122, *Weather massage*. Here, too, one player lies on his stomach with his eyes closed. The person lying down is declared to be a 'pizza', ready for the toppings. First, the four pizza bakers have to firmly 'knead' the dough, represented by the back of the person being massaged. Then the dough has to be rolled out: the bakers have to stroke their friend's back with their palms. Then the toppings can be added by massaging the back using gentle pummelling movements. The first baker puts ham on the pizza; the second, pepperoni; the third might break an egg over the pizza; while the fourth uses his index finger to push little olives into the dough. The upper and lower thighs could also be covered in toppings. Then the pizza has to go into the oven. For this phase, all of the pizza bakers place their hands on the back and legs of the person being massaged, who soaks up the warmth of the 'oven'. When he thinks he is 'done', he tells the others he is baked. Then the other people in the group take it in turns to be pizzas.

(124) Sensitive touch

Everyone in the group splits into pairs and player A lies on his back, closing his eyes, while B kneels down and puts his palms on A's stomach, leaving them there for a little while. During this time, B tries to become aware of his partner's breathing. Then, at intervals of about half a minute, B moves his hands to other places on A's body (forehead, shoulder, chest, legs, and feet). Then the roles are swapped.

(125) Musical meditation

The room should be darkened as much as possible at the beginning of this exercise, by turning off the lights and drawing the curtains. The players lie down comfortably on the floor and close their eyes. The group leader now plays a tape or CD of relaxing music. After approximately 20 minutes, the group leader slowly turns the music down and eventually off.

Afterwards, the players should be given the opportunity to gradually return to reality from their meditative state. It is important that the room remains dark during this phase, and that everybody is allowed to decide when they want to open their eyes and sit up. To finish, individual players may wish to talk about how the meditation has worked for them, but this should be on a voluntary basis only.

Materials: tape recorder/CD player, tape/CD of relaxing music. Any good record store will have a wide selection of relaxing music.

126 Story meditation

At the same time as the *Musical meditation* described in game 125, the group leader can tell one or several short stories suitable for relaxation.

Materials: tape recorder/CD player, tape/CD of relaxing music. Relaxing stories.

Conscious breathing

After the room has been darkened and all of the players are lying on the floor, the group leader begins the breathing meditation.

> 'Start to focus on your breathing. Breathe in and out slowly and evenly and, while doing so, try to consciously feel your breathing.'

The group leader lets a minute or so pass, during which she reminds the players one more time to breathe in and out, slowly and deliberately.

> 'Now imagine that you let the air you are breathing out flow into your right foot, rather than out of your body.'

She waits for approximately half a minute, then continues:

> 'Notice how your foot has slowly filled up with your breath. Now let the breath flow up into your right, lower thigh, just as deliberately and evenly.'

This exercise continues with the leader giving a new instruction after every 30 to 40 seconds.

> 'When you can feel that your lower thigh has filled with your breath, let the breath continue to flow up into your upper thigh until it, too, has filled up with air.

> 'Now breathe slowly and evenly into the right side of your pelvis.

'Now breathe into the left side of your pelvis until your whole pelvis is filled with breath.

'Now let the breath flow from the left side of your pelvis into your left, upper thigh.

'Your breath now continues to flow from your left, upper thigh further down into your lower thigh.

'Now your breath flows into your left foot.

'When the lower part of your body has filled with breath, let it flow into each individual finger of your right hand ... into your right, lower arm ... into your right, upper arm ... into your right shoulder ... from there into your stomach ... from there, the flow of breath moves upwards into your chest ... then into your left shoulder ... into your left, upper arm ... into the left, lower arm ... into each individual finger of your left hand ...

'Now try once more consciously to feel how you have received your breath throughout your body. While you do this, continue to breathe slowly and evenly.'

After a certain time, the group leader asks the players slowly to open their eyes and sit up gradually. Afterwards, the players can reflect on the exercise as a group: who was able to go along with this exercise, and who found it more difficult?

(128) I can do that!

This exercise can be used to end a meeting, seminar or workshop. In this case, all of the players (as long as they are prepared to do so) can participate in the game.

Every human being possesses skills that they have perfected to a greater degree than many other people in their environment. This game is about bringing their own particular skills to the attention of the other members of the group.

A volunteer stands in the middle and, first of all, tells everybody what he can do best. For example, Rita might claim, 'I am a good rider'. Then she describes to the others how she carries out this activity, starting with tacking up her horse, then riding out and, finally, caring for the horse afterwards.

This activity can also be used at the end of a theatre rehearsal. In that case, only one person volunteers, and then another person can have a turn at the end of the next rehearsal, so that the exercise stretches over several weeks.

(129) Singing canon

Singing canon with the whole group can form a nice conclusion to a seminar or workshop. There is a large choice of canons available, for example, 'Go down Moses', 'Frère Jacques', and so on.

Materials: canon books (available to buy or order from most good bookshops)

(130) Group leader's questionnaire

Exercises 130 to 135 are less suited to closing a rehearsal, but are good for concluding a longer or more intense period of work, such as a seminar or workshop. Just before the end of the seminar, the group leader hands out questionnaires to all of the players, and the group members have to briefly reflect on these, before commenting one at a time. Sample questions might include:

1 Did the seminar meet my personal expectations?
2 How did I feel about the group at the beginning of the seminar?
3 How do I feel about the group now?
4 Which exercises did I find particularly helpful?
5 Which exercises were less helpful for me?
6 From my point of view, was there a distinct breakthrough moment?
7 Were there any areas or issues that I would have liked to have spent more time on?
8 Would I be interested in a continuation of this programme?
9 What could be improved for next time?
10 How can I apply what I have learned in the seminar/workshop into everyday life?
11 How am I going to interact with the group after this seminar?
12 Have I also learned something about myself? If so, what?

13 Was I satisfied with the performance of the group leader?

For this activity, it is very important that all of the players are honest in their feedback. Even answers which, at first sight, may appear negative, should be received factually and never personally – of course, this also implies that the answers are phrased appropriately.

(131) Wishing tree

The group leader cuts out a tree from a large sheet of paper, such as a roll of wallpaper. The tree should be at least two metres high and should have numerous branches and twigs. Because this tree is a wishing tree, it will be hung with wishes and not fruit. The players are responsible for hanging their own wishes. Every group member takes paper and cuts out the shape of a fruit such as an apple, a pear or an orange, about the size of a small plate. On one side of the fruit the players use coloured pens to write their wishes for the group's future. The type of wish is left to each individual: for example, they could wish for inner peace, a rainbow, lots of positive energy, light-heartedness, and so on.

After everybody has written down their wishes on the pieces of fruit, these are stuck to the branches and twigs of the wishing tree, using glue. Then the tree is spread out on the floor in front of the whole group, so that everybody can read what their fellow group members have wished for themselves and the group. This game should definitely *not* be followed by subsequent reflection. Everyone can absorb and take home the wishes from the wishing tree that particularly appeal to them.

Materials: long piece of paper (eg. wallpaper), scissors, glue, lots of coloured pens

Picture of desire

The good wishes of individual members for the whole group can also be presented in the form of a picture. For this, a large sheet of paper is spread out on the floor. Everybody equips themselves with coloured pens and begins to draw. How they portray their wishes is up to each individual. Again, at the end, the picture should *not* be discussed, but everybody could pick out specific wishes for themselves instead.

Materials: paper, lots of coloured pens

(133) Laying on hands to say goodbye

This exercise can only be carried out with a small group or, when working with a large group, with individual players, because otherwise it will be too time-consuming. Player A goes into the middle of the room and closes his eyes. The others form a circle around him. Another person leaves the circle, walks up to A and places his right hand somewhere on A's body (his shoulder, head, arm, or stomach), letting it rest there. Then the next person steps forward and places his hand on another part of A's body. One after the other, the remaining people in the circle step forward and place one hand on A, until everybody has one hand resting on A. Player A takes in the individual touches without opening his eyes. He feels the contact and warmth from the others and tries to take home some of that feeling.

One at a time, the others let go of A and, once again, form a circle around him. When the last person has taken their hand away and has stepped back into the circle, A opens his eyes. He can describe briefly how he felt during this exercise. Then, if there is time, another person can request to have hands laid on him.

(134) Farewell looks

At the beginning of this exercise, two players at a time stand opposite each other. They stare fixedly into each other's eyes without saying a word. Using only their eyes, they say goodbye to each other. After about half a minute, everyone swaps partners, until each person has said goodbye to everyone else, using only their eyes. Then everybody stands in a circle and holds hands. The whole group remains standing in this position for a certain amount of time and everybody once more lets their eyes wander across the faces of the other players, without speaking. To finish off, they all squeeze the hands of their neighbours on the right and left, then the circle quietly dissolves.

Parting round with stone

A stone can be used for a closing round, as well as an opening round. For this activity, the group sits in a circle again and the group leader passes a stone from hand to hand around the circle of players. The person who has ownership of the stone can comment on the meeting, seminar or rehearsal. Did it meet their expectations? How did he find the individual exercises, the group, or the group leader, and so on? Again, the same rule as before applies: only the person holding the stone may speak, while the others have to listen carefully.

Materials: stone (fist sized)

Special Exercises & Tips for Amateur Dramatics Groups

The following exercises are particularly suitable for amateur dramatics groups at the start of a production, when the players are beginning to rehearse a particular play. The exercises can be used to explore the play to be rehearsed, and, while working through them, the actors are given the opportunity to study and develop their own parts in detail. During this phase, both general exercises, as well as targeted questions about the personality of a character, can be helpful.

Before the various exercises relating to the play or its characters are tackled, a number of different questions need to be considered, primarily which play the group is going to perform. Once the play has been decided, the next problem is what to bear in mind when casting the different roles.

This last chapter is a guide for the group leader or producer trying to answer these questions. The more conscientious a group leader or producer is in dealing with these issues prior to starting rehearsals, the greater the chances that the production will be a success.

136 Key questions regarding role and character biography

Once every member has been assigned their role, it is time to start looking into character biographies – in other words, to research the characters each is going to portray. This should not be the task of the producer alone, since it is far more helpful if each actor starts to form his own thoughts about his role. To do this, the group leader could put together a list of questions applicable to each role. These questions are handed out to all of the players on sheets of paper, with enough space under each question for the players to write their own comments. At the next meeting the group gets together and everybody presents the answers relating to their own roles and discusses whether the responses are appropriate to the roles. The questionnaires could cover the following ground:

Basic questions

1 What is my name?
2 How old am I?
3 What do I look like?
4 Do I have physical or psychological impairments?
5 How do I make a living?
6 In what sort of environment do I live and socialise?
7 In real life, what is my attitude to the social circle with which I am involved during the play?
8 Can I sketch out my character, using the minimum number of words?

9 Am I satisfied with my circumstances? (Be quite specific, if necessary.)

10 What sort of mood am I in at the beginning of the play?

11 What motivates my actions?

12 What is my function in the play/scene?

More detailed questions

13 What is the main theme of my role?

14 Over what sort of (historical) time-scale is my role played out?

15 What has my character's life been like so far?

16 Where am I in the play, with regard to time (time of day, season)?

17 What sort of sensory stimuli is my character experiencing?

18 How am I going to interact with people in the different scenes, and how am I going to utilise props?

19 What does my character expect from life and his environment?

20 Where and how in the play does the expected come true? What do I do to satisfy my desires?

21 What relationships are there between different people or objects in the play?

22 How do these relationships affect the embodiment of my role?

23 How does the locality and atmosphere change through the performance of my own and other roles?

24 Where are turning points created? Perhaps by new people or objects coming onto the scene?

25 What are the most outstanding positive and negative personality traits of my character?

26 Which animal would go with my role – a courageous lion, a proud peacock, a faithful dog, or something else?

27 Has the role got any comical aspects? What are they?

28 Is there something that my character would normally never do that, in the course of the play, he ends up doing nevertheless (even if only in a small way)?

29 Is there a movement or an expression that my character keeps using?

30 In what sort of mood do I finish the play?

In order not to overwhelm the actors with this list of questions, the group leader could hand out the first 12 questions to start with, or she could select certain questions and put together a list for each individual. Questions 13 to 30, which go into a lot more detail, can be handed out during later rehearsals. Overall, this questionnaire method has the advantage that the players themselves will spend time thinking about their roles, rather than leaving this to the group leader. The alternative method is for the group leader to explain to each actor why he must act in a certain way. However, a role is generally acted out much more credibly if the actor has worked out for himself why he is acting in a certain way, in a specific situation, during the course of the play.

(137) Pronunciation practice

Pronunciation is an important aspect of dramatics. It does not matter how well a play is acted and how convincing the actors are – all these efforts are in vain if the audience is unable to understand what the actors are saying. In order to create a greater awareness of the clarity of one's own pronunciation, several scenes could be selected from the play that is currently being rehearsed. These are acted out as usual, but the players have to stick a cork between their front teeth at the beginning of the rehearsal. The other players have to take part, not merely as an audience, but also as active listeners. They can then give the actors feedback about which parts can be understood, in spite of the unclear pronunciation, as well as sections in which pronunciation must be improved in order for the audience to be able to understand what is going on.

(138) Sentences in different moods

Each player chooses a sentence which, in his opinion, has a special significance for the character he is playing. Then each actor repeats his sentence using different moods: for example, sadly, happily, courageously, fearfully, bitterly, hurriedly, monotonously, excitedly, angrily, aggressively, shyly, wearily, alertly, and so on. In this way, he can find out for himself which intonation or mood would best suit the sentence and the character of the person to be portrayed. If necessary, feedback can be sought from the group to make sure the actors have got it right.

(139) Developing characters (2)

This is a variation on Game 114, *Developing characters (1)* (p133). In this exercise, once again, the players are required to work out body posture and life story for a role (if necessary, with appropriate headgear), this time specifically for the character they are portraying in the current play.

Materials: large number of different hats

(140) Scene exit (2)

This is a variation on Game 100, *Scene exit (1)* (p114). In this exercise, the group leader and the actor choose a scene from the text to be studied. The player, together with his fellow actors, now acts out the scene and, at certain places, interrupts the play and steps out of the scene. Then he comments on the scene and describes his feelings. As the experience is not his own, his perceptions should not be described from a personal point of view, but in the words of the person he embodies during that scene. This exercise can help actors to gain more insight into why their characters in the play might be behaving in certain ways.

(141) Incorporating body postures into a scene (2)

This is a variation on Game 102, *Incorporating body postures into a scene (1)* (p116). A group of actors whose characters encounter each other during the play currently being rehearsed tries out different body postures (three per person), which are, in the opinion of these individuals, compatible with the roles they embody. Then they act out part of a scene where they all appear together. During the course of the scene, each actor incorporates the body postures he has previously worked on. Afterwards, the group reflects on whether or not each body posture suits the character for whom it was chosen. If not, was this because of the personality of the character, or because of the situation in which the character found himself during the course of the scene?

142　Character raffle

The group leader determines an outstanding character trait for each figure in the play that is currently being studied. Then she gives the characters last names, according to these traits. For example:

♦ A person who only talks about himself in the play is named Mr Important.

♦ A person who is extremely moody is called Mr Grumpy.

♦ A person who always generates good morale and happiness is called Mr Sunshine.

♦ A person who is particularly shy or inhibited could be Mr Don't-touch-me.

♦ A person who has a very condescending manner is called Mr High-and-mighty.

This exercise demands creativity from the group leader, since she must use her imagination to think of names relating to the different characters. The invented names are then written on separate pieces of paper which are each put into their own envelope. Then the group leader gathers together everyone who has a role in the play. Each player randomly chooses an envelope, takes it and reads the imaginary name written on it.

Then comes the most important part of the exercise, during which the group leader holds back and simply functions as a neutral observer. It is now the task of the players to work out, through discussion, whether or not they have picked a name that suits their characters. If, as is most likely, they have not, the players have to swap the pieces of paper around until the group agrees that everybody has got the last name which goes with their own character. Finally, everybody should provide a brief reason why they think that their role suits that name.

Materials: pieces of paper, envelopes, pen

Projecting emotions into a different situation

The group leader chooses those feelings that are of particular significance during the course of the play currently being rehearsed. She then provides the participating players with a new scenario in which these same feelings have to be acted out. The players then try to portray the feelings that they normally represent in the play in these new situations. For example, the group might be rehearsing a play in which two people are linked by fate. Person A is ill and dependent on constant care from person B. In other words, A is in the hands of B. The crucial feelings in this scene are *helplessness* (A) and *power* (B).

A and B are then given a new situation by the group leader, in which they have to act out the relationship and feelings from the previous scene. A is now an employee who makes a crucial mistake at work and has to own up to B, his employer. B has to exercise his authority, since A's existence is more or less in B's hands. A, on the other hand, has to express his helplessness, because he is reliant on his job and is, therefore, dependent on B's goodwill as his employer.

Materials: props if necessary

144 Projecting people into a different situation

In order to gain more insight into the personality of a particular dramatic character, the actor can also try to get to know this 'person' outside of the play. For this exercise, the group leader asks the individuals in the play to pretend to meet each other in situations totally unrelated to those in the play. In contrast to game 143, players do not simply carry over their relationships and feelings to another dramatic scene, but they actually attempt to act out the same role as they have in the original play.

The play to be studied is about a social evening, with two married couples in attendance. The first married couple, who are very bourgeois, have invited the other couple for dinner. The second (invited) couple are, in contrast, very well to do. Accordingly, tensions arise between the two couples. At this point the group leader moves away from the script and has the two couples meeting, not at the house of the first couple, but in different places: for example, a kebab van, an elevator, a lady's toilet during a club social, at the theatre or the cinema, during a flight, at a supermarket, and so on.

The group leader and the actors can now observe whether or not the significant personality traits of the characters can be carried over to a different location and a different situation. Who was convincing during this improvisation and stayed in role? Who is still too attached to the situation that is prescribed by the play, finding it difficult to leave this behind?

Materials: props if necessary

(145) Flashback

Each play has a beginning and an ending – obviously! But what might have happened between the characters before the play actually started? The group leader asks the players to portray their characters in the moods they experienced just before the action of the play started. Try using the two couples from Game 144 again.

The play begins with all four people sitting at the table having a meal. As if in a flashback, the players now have to act out what, in their view, might have happened between the two couples just before they met for dinner. We already know that neither couple was particularly keen to meet. First it is the less well-off couple's turn: the two players act out a scene taking place approximately half an hour before the expected guests arrived. Both are busy getting dressed, laying the table, preparing the meal, and so on. However, it is not just their actions that are relevant, but, more importantly, the feelings that both are experiencing at that time. They have to make it obvious how nervous and unsure they feel about the forthcoming event. After that, the more privileged couple gets dressed up for their evening out: in this situation, the actors have to make it plain that the couple are not particularly looking forward to going out, since they see their hosts as rather 'beneath' them.

Materials: props if necessary

146 Credits

In principle, this exercise is very similar to Game 145, *Flashback*. However, this time, the actors do not act out what happened before the beginning of the play, but what happens after the play is over. For example, the original play ended with both couples having a huge argument. The visiting couple stormed out of their hosts' house, and the hosts were left behind, feeling frustrated.

Then, in free improvisation, the individual players act out what might have happened between the participating figures after the end of the play. The host couple now sit at the table, feeling flattened and blaming each other for the disastrous end to the evening they had planned so well. The visitors, on the other hand, confirm to each other on their way home that they had known right from the beginning that this evening was going to be a flop. If possible, Game 145, *Flashback*, and Game 146, *Credits*, should be played one after the other. In this way, the actors can clarify the following issues: in what mood do I enter the play? In what sort of mood do I leave the play? What is the drive or motivation behind my actions during the play? Which point or scene is the decisive factor for determining that the play ends in the way it does?

By linking the two exercises and the resulting questions, everybody can discover where their actions in the play ultimately lead, and how their feelings change in the course of the play.

(147) Checklist for selecting a play

The following points may serve as a checklist when selecting a suitable play. This important decision is obviously crucial, because the play that is finally chosen will build the focus for group work in the weeks or months to come.

1 If, to start with, the group has not decided on a particular play or project, it needs to consider getting hold of a selection of potential scripts. In order to get an insight into what is on offer, try ordering catalogues from the leading theatrical publishing companies; many now also provide access to their products via the internet. Some theatrical publishers even focus on work for amateur dramatics groups.

2 Each script that makes it through the initial selection process should first be read without interpretation or casting. Who is going to play which role is not important at this point in time; instead, the play as a whole should be the main focus. Equally unimportant is whether the play is to be read by one person, or an entire group.

3 Readers should reflect on the images and associations that are conjured up while reading the script.

4 If there are several scripts in the final selection, one person or several people could research the historic, social and political backgrounds of each play.

5 Information about the author could be collected.

6 The players could look for scripts that have a similar theme.

7 Everybody could ask themselves how a potential play concerns them personally: 'Which actions have I experienced myself or can I relate to?'

8 The group leader or director, together with volunteers from the group, could gather together literature about the play (if available) and look into the play in more detail.

9 What demands is the play going to make, in terms of acting skills? Does the group have the quantitative and qualitative potential demanded by this play?

10 What technical requirements does the play have, and will it be possible to realise them using the resources available to the group?

11 What sort of requirements in terms of equipment (backdrops, costumes, etc) does the play have, and will it be possible to realise them using the resources available to the group?

12 What costs will be involved, in terms of equipment and royalties?

13 Will it be possible to put on the play within the time available to the group?

14 What sort of audience is the play going to appeal to – children? Teenagers? Young adults? Or older people?

15 In addition, the group should check the plays that are being put on by other amateur or professional theatre groups in the area, in order to avoid staging an identical play at the same time.

(148) Key points for casting

The following questions could be useful when selecting actors for particular roles:

1 Will it be possible to assign a person to each role, or will it be necessary or advisable to assign more than one role to a particular actor (ie, one person plays two, or several, small roles)?

2 If there is a difference between the numbers of male and female actors available, and the numbers of male and female roles which need to be assigned in a favoured play, is it possible to rewrite some roles to suit the gender of actors available?

3 Would it be possible for some of the women in the group to take on male roles? Of course, men could also play female roles, but this tends to work best in a comedy.

4 If there is a shortage of actors, is it possible to cut out some of the less important 'extras' from the play?

5 If there are too many actors, would it be possible to add one, or several, small roles to the play? Remember that this might first need to be agreed with the publisher or playwright, depending on who holds the copyright for the play in question.

6 Which role suits which group member best, in terms of physical attributes (appearance, voice, etc) and character?

7 Are the people playing the lead roles flexible, for

example, in terms of having to attend additional rehearsals? Have they any talent for improvisation, in case something goes wrong during a performance?

8 Are the people intended for main roles sufficiently reliable with regard to their regular presence at rehearsals, as well as the amount of time and effort required?

9 Are there any individuals in the group who might benefit from the experiment of giving them a role that, at first sight, is exactly the opposite of their real character?

10 If several people are possible contenders for a lead role, the director might think of choosing the person who, in the past, has only played smaller roles. In this way, different players get the chance to prove their skills in a larger role.